IF YOU **WANT SOMETHING** YOU HAVE TO **SAY SOMETHING**

Learn how to
UNLOCK the Secret Power
of the **TONGUE**
to receive
YOUR HEARTS DESIRES

DR. SHAUN MARLER

Copyright Page

If You Want Something, You Have to Say Something

The Secret Power of Your Tongue Receive Your Heart's Desires and Have Your Needs Met

© 2025 Dr Shaun Marler

Published by: World Harvest Ministries

PO Box 90, Bald Hills
QLD Australia 4036

All rights reserved. No part of this publication may be reproduced, stored in a retrieval system, or transmitted in any form or by any means electronic, mechanical, photocopying, recording, or otherwise without the prior written permission of the publisher, except as permitted by the Copyright Act 1968 (Cth) or for the purposes of review, criticism, or academic study.

Scripture quotations are from KJV, unless otherwise stated. Used by permission. All rights reserved.

This book is intended for informational and inspirational purposes only. The author and publisher disclaim any liability for any loss or damage resulting from reliance on the information contained herein.

National Library of Australia Cataloguing-in-Publication Data:

[ISBN: 9780648589792]

Christian Living, General, Personal Growth, Spiritual Growth

Printed and bound in Australia.

For permissions and inquiries, contact:

World Harvest Ministries

general@whm.org.au

If You Want Something, You Have To Say Something

*The secret power of your tongue
- receive your heart's desires
and have your needs met*

In this book you will learn:

1. That death and life is in the power of your tongue
2. God has given you a choice: choose life or death, blessing or the curse
3. How to unlock the secret power of your tongue
4. The importance of right or wrong thinking
5. Strategies to win in life
6. God's Will is prosperity, peace and wellbeing
7. Insights into your Abrahamic inheritance
8. A major key to unlock Heaven's victories
9. That words are seeds
10. How to sow words to reap rewards
11. How words can affect your mental health
12. God's Word System, and His original plan for all people!
13. That the testimony of Jesus, is the Spirit of prophecy
14. Your words define your dreams or destroy them

This is a must have book, that is based on and filled with scripture from God's Word. It's an introduction into the secret power of words and how to use them for your benefit. It's a how-to book, your future self will thank you for taking the time to read this book!

Contents

Dedication	6
Acknowledgement	7
Preface	8
Introduction	11
Chapter 1: The Secret Power Of The Tongue	13
Chapter 2: The Word Regulates Our Life For Success	19
Chapter 3: God's Word System	27
Chapter 4: Dominion	45
Chapter 5: Imitate God	55
Chapter 6: Jesus operated This Way!	61
Chapter 7: Sow The Word	69
Chapter 8: What You See in Your Mind Comes To Pass In Time	75
Chapter 9: A Vision With Purpose	87
Chapter 10: Decree As A king	103
Chapter 11: Intimacy	119
Chapter 12: Angels Operate This Way	127
Chapter 13: Confessing God's Word	135
Chapter 14: Frequency	147
Chapter 15: A Bold Challenge - Don Gossett	165
Chapter 16: Great Achievements	169
Chapter 17: Don't Quit!	187
Chapter 18: Abraham's Seed	195
Chapter 19: If It's To Be It's Up To Me!	201
Chapter 20: Who Am I In Christ	219
Chapter 21: Daily Affirmations	227
A Guide To Salvations	235

Dedication

This book is dedicated to every person who desires to win in life through Jesus Christ and who desire to enter into the fullness of His plans and purposes for their life.

Acknowledgement

I would like to acknowledge and thank every person that has helped me in bringing this book to print. A big thank you to Christopher and Jessica Hockridge, who without their tireless work, great suggestions and input, editing, typing, setting and design, and helping me, without which, I would not have been able to get this book into your hands.

I would also like to thank, my wife Kerrie Marler, and my family for all their support, input, and prayers. And especially my daughter Cherise Marler, for helping create the cover design and her many suggestions.

I would also like to thank the members of World Harvest Ministries and friends who have also read drafts and given valuable feedback for the layout and cover design. Once again, a big thank you to everybody that has supported World Harvest Ministries and the dream that God has placed in my heart to reach people with His Word and His love. Your faithfulness in partnership, prayers, encouragement, and finances has helped to inspire me to continue and fulfil my God given mandate.

Most of all I want to thank the Lord Jesus Christ for calling me into His service.

May God bless you all,
Ps Shaun

Preface

For many years, I have studied and taught on confessing the Word and the power of the tongue. I remember, years ago, when my good friend Don Gossett (author of over 120 books) came and ministered at my Church in Brisbane, Australia, that he called me up at the end and said, *"Shaun, I want to pray for you."*

He laid his hands upon me, and said, *"I'm imparting a blessing upon your life. Hold out your hands."* Then, he took my hands, and as he held them he said, *"I pray and declare, you are anointed for the write stuff!"*

It was a play on words. He was imparting the anointing that he operated in to me, to write books.

From that time, I have had a great desire to write books. I have personally prayed to the Lord to give me books that would be a blessing to those that read them and applied the truths and the revelations from God's Word, revealed therein; touching and making a difference, blessing their lives and families.

I believe, that this book is one such book and if you take it, study it, and apply it, the truths that you will discover herein, that I've revealed, will bless you and put your life on a road to success.

Being a partner with Jesse Duplantis Ministries, one day I received a CD in the mail, titled, *Give God A Job.* As I listened to that CD over and over, Jesse kept reiterating that if you wanted something from God, you have to say something. As I listened to Jesse expand the Word, that saying went off in my spirit. I thought of all of the great men and women of God whose works I have studied and researched along with the Bible over the years who have preached on the power of the tongue. Mighty men of God like, Kenneth Copeland, E.W. Kenyan, Jerry Savelle, Lester Sumrall, Drummond Thom, to mention but a few.

I prayed and I gave God a job, *"Father, by the power of the Holy Spirit and in the name of Jesus Christ, Lord, please empower me and help me to produce a book on the secret power of the tongue, as revealed by your Spirit through your Word."*

This is how this work came to fruition. God has also provided me with wonderful, skilful people who have helped me to produce this work to get it into your hands. If you like this work and want to help me produce more teachings and books, and bring this work to seeking people all over the world, you can do so by becoming a partner with our ministry. Details to become a partner are in the back of the book.

I encourage you to dive in, study, meditate, absorb, and apply the teachings and instructions that you will find in this book and put your life on a road to success.

Introduction

Everyone desires a better life. Regardless of your current situation or identity, you have hopes and dreams. People continually look forward to a brighter future for themselves, their children, families, and the world. There is an inherent, in-built drive in every living being to grow and increase. It's the law of the seed.

In Genesis 1:11, the Bible says: *"And God said, Let the earth bring forth grass, the herb yielding seed, and the fruit tree yielding fruit after his kind, whose seed is in itself, upon the earth: and it was so."*

God explains that every seed produces fruit of its kind and has a natural urge to multiply and grow. From a single apple seed, we can grow an apple tree with numerous apples, each containing more seeds. God has designed every seed to reproduce itself many times over.

You and I are created in God's image. In 1 Peter 1:23, it is written that we are born again of incorruptible seed by the living and enduring Word of God. God's Word is seed. Jesus Christ Himself was the Word and seed of God. He was Abraham's seed, sent to bring forth God's life in us. This life emerges as we let God's Word take root in our hearts.

It takes root when we believe, confess, and affirm that Jesus is the Son of God who came in the flesh, died for us, and rose again. By receiving Him and confessing Him as our Lord and Saviour, we are born again! We are transformed—a new creation in Christ. Now, through the same Word, we are to go forth, speak it, and bring forth life and fruit for God.

Jesus told us that He is the vine and we are the branches (John 15:5). The Father is glorified as we produce fruit for His glory through His Word and name. The Word serves as a guide—a plumb line, a rule, and a law. By obeying, following, and applying the principles in God's Word to our lives, families, and businesses, we can guide them toward success.

It was C.S. Lewis, the great author, who said, *"You are never too old to set another goal or to dream a new dream."*

Your new goal or dream starts in your imagination and then is spoken into manifestation through the words of your mouth.

Chapter One:

The Secret Power of the Tongue

"For as a man think in his heart, so is he."
— **Proverbs 23:7A**

To transform your life, you must transform your thoughts, actions, and words. Change the way you think and speak, and you will change the way you live.

"If you want something you've never had, you have to do something you've never done!"

This is a saying I've been sharing and writing about for nearly forty years. Many have embraced it, using its wisdom to progress in their lives, careers, or pursuits. When it comes to the power of words, I often say, *"If you want something, you have to say something!"* Perhaps it's something you've never said before. I believe in speaking the powerful Word of

God over your life. Declare the promises in God's Word—promises Jesus secured for you with His life and blood on the cross of Calvary. Through faith in Him, you've become an heir to all God has promised. It's time to seize it! Don't be afraid to try something new or say something you've never said. Embrace the hidden power of your words!

God has established laws, both natural and supernatural, that govern the universe, including both the visible and invisible realms. These laws, along with words, shape our world. We have the natural laws we are familiar with; like those of biology, chemistry, mathematics, physics, as well as a law of health etc. Many years ago, Wallace D. Wattles wrote a book on another law, which he referred to as the science of getting rich. In it, Wattles contends that wealth is an exact science, more on this later. There are also spiritual laws, one of these being the law of death and life. Romans 8:2 states: *"For the law of the Spirit of life in Christ Jesus has made me free from the law of sin and death."*

God has set laws to oversee His entire creation, both visible and invisible. The laws of death and life, blessing and curses, are activated by the power of the tongue (Deuteronomy 30:19). I have a saying that I've used many times in my preaching, *"The Word works when you work the Word."*

The Secret Power Of The Tongue

The Word works when you work the Word

Today, your words are either working for you or against you. Laws concerning your life, future, family, business, and destiny are in motion. You might not consider yourself a creative being, but you are! You were created in the image of a perfect God, and God is a creator. He has given you the remarkable ability to create with words—through the power of your tongue—the future and the things you desire to see in this life and the next.

We need to walk by faith in the direction of our dreams and desires. All achievements first start with a desire. Desires are formed within us through our thought life, imagination, and words—what we say, read, or continually dwell on. These things can either feed our destiny or starve it. Many years ago, I read a book about the power of imagination and how thoughts are like clouds, that go out and gather up results for us. Have you ever suddenly thought about someone you hadn't considered in a while, only to run into them, get a phone call, or see them soon after? It all started with a thought. Thoughts are incredibly powerful, and our thought life is influenced by what we focus on and talk about—what we read, see, and imagine. These elements have significant implications for our daily lives.

Proverbs 23:7A states: *"For as a man thinks in his heart, so is he."*

The Way You Think, And What You Think, Is Important

What are you thinking about in your heart today? What is your heart's desire? Whatever it is, it matters. In Luke 6:45, Jesus said: *"A good man out of the good treasure of his heart brings forth that which is good; and an evil man out of the evil treasure of his heart brings forth that which is evil: for out of the abundance of the heart his mouth speaks."*

In this scripture, the Greek word for heart, *kardia*, signifies more than just the physical organ that circulates blood. It encompasses the thoughts and feelings of the mind and is considered the centre of both spiritual and physical life. Jesus illustrates that our thought life can lead to the creation of good or bad things.

Isaiah 57:19 states: *"I create the fruit of the lips; Peace, peace to him that is far off, and to him that is near, says the LORD; and I will heal him."*

This passage reveals that God is the creator of the fruit of your lips. This is because of a law He established when He created the Earth. As long as this Earth exists, the law of seedtime and harvest will continue. The seeds you plant through your words will yield a harvest. If you are unhappy with the harvest your words are producing, you must alter your thoughts in your heart and your manner of speaking.

This law—the power of the tongue—works for everyone, both saved and unsaved. No matter where you live, God has invested power in people's tongues. That power is released through spoken words. Everything you need to have a successful life is in the Word of God. Once you are born again, everything you need to transform your world is within you.

Jesus said that the kingdom of God is within you (Luke 17:21). You possess everything you need to transform your dreams into realities. You are a person of infinite worth and unique possibilities, endowed with the seeds of greatness and designed for accomplishment and engineered for success. You are God's Plan A. He loves you and sent His Son to die for you. God has a loving and great plan for your life, and He doesn't have a Plan B. You are it! You are somebody! God doesn't waste His time creating nobodies, you were made by God. You are one of a kind—the only one of you God has.

By using words, you can cultivate an attitude of gratitude and thanksgiving towards God daily for creating you and providing you with the keys to His Word to make you a winner in life. An attitude of gratitude and thanksgiving, expressed through the power of words, will be a channel for your wealth to come. I like to say: *"It's absolutely essential to have an attitude of gratitude and to say and speak the right things."*

This will draw the right people and favourable circumstances into your life. Gratitude and thanksgiving expressed through words will lift you out of the pitfalls and attacks of the enemy during challenging seasons. This positive power of God, released through the spoken Word, will cause you to rise—rise above all circumstances. There is no better way to express gratitude than through positive, life-giving words of love, faith, hope, and appreciation.

Chapter Two:

The Word Regulates Our Life For Success

"Study this Book of Instruction continually. Meditate on it day and night so you will be sure to obey everything written in it. Only then will you prosper and succeed in all you do."
— **Joshua 1:8 NLT**

The Word regulates your life for success. Whatever your dream, you must plant the vision with God's Word and the promises it holds. Every purpose and vision you connect to in life will have scripture that assures you of the performance of that promise.

First, gather information from God's Word, then meditate on it. Through meditation of the information that you have gathered, you can begin to create a picture in your imagination of that goal or dream. Write down this vision, dream, or goal and the steps you are going to take to achieve them. These steps will come to you or be revealed to you, by God's Spirit. Keep them visible and speak them out, declaring them in the name of Jesus as if they are already manifested.

The Seed Is Not Sown In Your Heart Until You Understand It

The seed isn't sown in your heart until you understand it! Through meditation, you plant that seed in your heart or spirit. By faith, you see your desire already manifested in the spirit with the eyes of your spirit.

What you envision in your mind will come to pass in time. Meditation helps build the image of victory, desire, or achievement in your inner man— your spirit man. Then by faith, you declare it into the natural world. The Word is a seed that produces fruit after its kind. From the Bible or God's Word, we receive the information or seed needed to sow in our heart. Through meditation, your heart or inner man receives a revelation that the promise in the Word belongs to you. As you pray over your vision and dream, both in the natural and supernatural (praying in tongues, words taught by the Holy Spirit), you are watering the seed now sown in your heart. As you water that seed, it cracks open, and the life within it begins to grow and expand.

In nature, planting a seed and watering it is the beginning of a miraculous journey. As it sprouts, it pushes through the Earth's surface, and a tree starts to rise. With each passing day, branches unfurl from the trunk, giving birth to leaves and fruit, each packed with more seeds. Birds flock to these branches, finding shelter and nourishment in the fruit and seeds, which are the very essence of life.

In our own lives, planting God's Word (seed) in our heart and nurturing it through prayer, speaking in tongues, and affirming it is our way of taking charge. We wield authority over the weeds and enemies—those pesky thoughts and feelings—that try to stifle its growth. We stand firm against anything that contradicts our dreams and their path to reality. As we tend to this seed, it blossoms into a tree of revelation, its branches and fruit, or the manifestation of what we have sown and believed in, come to fruition.

The joy of this seed's fruit and blessings is yours to savour, but you can also share your testimonies with others, offering them the promises that have liberated you and brought you into His blessing. I pray that God's Holy Spirit grants you clarity and understanding of all this. The power, life, and strength within a seed can transform your life when allowed to flourish in your heart. God's Word will lead you to triumph.

Proverbs 29:18 in the Bible reminds us that without vision, people perish. It's vital to have a dream or vision for success in life—a dream to shine in your chosen field. Let a vision take root in your heart and spirit, inspired by God's Word and will. Then, boldly declare what you see in your spirit or mind's eye through your words, and believe it as if it were already a reality in the natural world.

God said to Joshua, *"I have given into your hand Jericho, and the king thereof, and the mighty men of valour."* (Joshua 6:2).

In the natural, Joshua could only see the towering walls and the soldiers stationed there. Yet, with the eyes of faith, Joshua was meant to envision these walls falling and he was to boldly declare that God had handed him the city. God desired that Joshua focus on the victory—the city and its king within his grasp. He was instructed to lead his army in a march around the walls of Jericho, sounding the trumpet of triumph. Through this act, he would claim the city, for the walls that stood in the natural realm, he saw them fall in the supernatural. What he envisioned with his spiritual eyes came to pass, and the walls collapsed in the natural. The people of God secured a monumental victory over Jericho, and Joshua seized the king and city.

The Word Regulates Our Life For Success

We inhabit a world brimming with words. How crucial they are! Words are like seeds. 1 Peter 1:23 states, *"Being born again, not of corruptible seed, but of incorruptible, by the Word of God, which lives and abides for ever."*

Without words, communication would be impossible. We use them to convey emotions, desires, love, compassion, and even hatred. Words are vital to us, as God reminds us in the Bible in Deuteronomy 30:19, we have the power to bless or curse with our own tongue. We are made in God's image, and just as He works through His Word system, He wants us to!

In truth, all of creation adheres to God's Word system. Even our human DNA is a sequence of encoded biological information that cells use to develop and function. DNA is a polymer composed of two polynucleotide chains that twist around each other to form a double helix. This polymer carries genetic instructions for the development, functioning, growth, and reproduction of all known organisms and many viruses.

We were crafted from the Earth's dust and brought to life by God's spoken Word. Our bodies are a marvel of deoxyribonucleic acid (DNA), a genetic code that makes each of us unique. DNA holds the blueprint for our development, growth, reproduction, and every function of life.

Creation itself was born from God's voice, and we were formed from the dust of the Earth, with God breathing His own life into us. When we are reborn, it's from that eternal seed, nurtured by God's Spirit, through His Word.

Declaring God's promises over your body, circumstances, and situations is wielding the very Word that created you and all of existence. By mirroring God, who spoke life and order into the chaos of Genesis 1:1-2, you can illuminate the darkness in your life. Just as God's Word restored order, light, and life to His creation, He has shown us we can also achieve this in our life. Through speaking His Word over our circumstances, they can be restored back to divine order, including; health, blessings, love, and life.

Remember, the power of your tongue shapes death and life! God now calls you to take authority and speak His peace-giving Word into any enemy attack, confusion, disorder, or disease around you. When you speak God's Word over yourself, you're inviting Him back into your life. God is the healer, repairer, and restorer of all things.

By speaking God's Word into any broken situation that you're facing, you're bringing creative light back to it and commanding the darkness to flee. In this way, God's Word guides your life to success.

The Word Regulates Our Life For Success

Today's Church is witnessing a surge in teachings about the words we speak. We're encouraged to confess the Word, stand firm on it, and speak solutions rather than problems. This focus is crucial: God is revealing that many of today's challenges stem from word curses. Curses are fuelled by incorrect thinking, which leads to wrong believing and then wrong speaking. A lot of people, without realising it, are verbally harming and cursing themselves, even to the point of self-destruction, with their own words.

However, others are transforming their lives, businesses, families, health, and any other form of captivity by changing their words. They have become conquerors instead of failures, prosperous instead of impoverished, and are beginning to enjoy the victorious living that Jesus Christ provided for them at Calvary.

"A man's belly shall be satisfied with the fruit of his mouth; and with the increase of his lips shall he be filled. Death and life are in the power of the tongue: and they that love it shall eat the fruit thereof" (Proverbs 18:20-21).

No matter your situation, you have the power to transform it by aligning with God's principles of life, liberty, and freedom.

What a profound declaration this scripture is! God has entrusted us with the power of life and death through our words. Consider this— He has literally given us such immense power.

My hope for you is that as we delve into this teaching from God's Word, your spiritual vision will be awakened, and you will gain profound truth and insight. I pray that by the power of the Holy Spirit, God will illuminate you and help you understand the incredible power of words, enabling you to use them wisely to positively alter your life's path!

Remember, in genesis chapter one, we see the first use of Words was for creation (Genesis 1:3) , not communication. The second use of Words was for communication (Genesis 1:26).

Chapter Three:

God's Word System

"I call heaven and earth to record this day against you, that I have set before you life and death, blessing and cursing: therefore choose life, that both you and your seed may live"
— **Deuteronomy 30:19**

Let's explore a few scriptures from the Word of God to understand how negative words can be harmful and destructive to our lives. Proverbs 18:21B tells us, *"Death and life are in the power of the tongue: and they that love it shall eat the fruit thereof."*

Words are incredibly powerful, capable of bringing both death and life. Unfortunately, people often use their words unwisely, causing harm to their families, businesses, relationships, and overall lives. I'm sure many of you have experienced the impact of words spoken to or about you.

This book aims to help you succeed in life by improving your words. It provides keys to empower yourself and your loved ones by speaking positive, life-giving words. We need to fill our hearts with hope and faith by speaking the Word of God and embracing its living, faith-filled promises. Let's read Proverbs 6:2 together: *"You are snared with the words of your mouth, you are taken with the words of your mouth."*

Proverbs 18:7 "A fool's mouth is his destruction, and his lips are the snare of his soul."

These two verses should be a wake-up call for us all! We need to understand the importance of our words. The term *"snare"* here originates from an old English word used by bird hunters, or fowlers, in England. They set traps for birds like pheasants and quails, using bait to lure them in. Once the bird took the bait with its beak, the trap would spring, catching the bird—which would then become lunch or dinner the next day!

In Proverbs 18:7, *"snare"* refers to a noose used to trap animals. When we reflect on these scriptures, we see that God vividly illustrates how harmful and destructive negative words can be to our lives and situations. Negative words can damage and ensnare our souls, much like a bird caught in a trap. This negative soul-tie, formed by ungodly and destructive words, can impact a person's mind, will, and emotions. These effects may persist for years until the curse of negative words is lifted, and the person is freed.

The good news is that every curse can be broken through the blood of Jesus, along with forgiveness and repentance. You can start today—this very minute! Begin transforming your life and future by speaking words of life, hope, and faith from God's Word. Remember, God is merciful and forgiving. Through repentance and forgiveness, and by the power of Jesus' blood, every negative word or verbal curse spoken over you can be removed and destroyed.

Nothing Happened Until God Spoke

Hebrews 11:3 says, *"Through faith we understand that the worlds were framed by the Word of God, so that things which are seen were not made of things which do appear."*

The entire universe, along with everything within it—both visible and invisible—was brought into existence by faith through God's spoken Word. This includes all spiritual principalities and powers, angels, fallen angels, and rebellious spirits, which we refer to as demons. As God spoke, the worlds and everything within them came into being.

You might wonder why God created Satan, fallen angels, and rebellious spirits, which seem to cause chaos in the world today. This topic will be explored in another book on spiritual warfare. However, briefly, when God created everything, it was good, as noted in Genesis 1. Even Satan was not initially created as an adversary. He was originally a beautiful archangel, designed to worship God and illuminate the universe with light, revelation, and insight.

God described him, saying, *"You were perfect in your ways from the day you were created, until sin and rebellion were found in you"* (Ezekiel 28:15).

The Bible reveals that Satan orchestrated a rebellion in Heaven, trying to overthrow God. Did you know He used words to achieve this? In Isaiah 14:4, it records Lucifer, who is Satan, as saying, *"I will ascend above the heights of the clouds; I will be like the Most High."*

Consider Deuteronomy 30:19:

"I call Heaven and Earth to record this day against you, that I have set before you life and death, blessing and cursing: therefore choose life, that both you and your seed may live."

Lucifer was initially created perfect, but his pride led him to rebel against God. He disobeyed God's Word and the divine order of good, beauty, and perfection. His pride fuelled jealousy and envy. Instead of being grateful for the skills, wisdom, and abilities God had bestowed upon him, he desired more and became self-entitled. His heart's desires were expressed through his words, inciting rebellion among one-third of Heaven's hosts.

Revelation 12:4 describes how he drew down *"one-third of the stars of heaven,"* referring to the angels who joined his rebellion. These rebellious words caused destruction in Heaven and on Earth. It's a sobering thought!

God warns us that, *"death and life are in the power of the tongue."* As illustrated in Deuteronomy 30:19–20, He grants us the free will to choose life or death, blessings or curses. This choice confronts us daily, and we can opt for life and blessings by speaking positive, faith-filled words from God's Word, accompanied by gratitude and thankfulness.

With blessings and curses before us, let us not emulate the rebellious angels who defied God. Instead, let us choose life and blessings, speaking faith-filled words with a grateful heart.

We choose life by meditating on positive thoughts and feeding our minds and spirits with uplifting words. We affirm this choice by carefully selecting the words we speak. As Jesus said, *"Out of the abundance of the heart, the mouth speaks"* (Luke 6:45). That's why I encourage you to cultivate a heart of praise and thanksgiving towards God by choosing the right words—words from His Word. Words of love, faith, praise, and thanksgiving. These life-giving words will benefit you and those who hear them, whether they are family or friends.

The Word in Ephesians 4:29 instructs us, *"Let no corrupt communication proceed out of your mouth, but that which is good to the use of edifying, that it may minister grace unto the hearers."*

In Job 6:25A, it highlights, *"How forcible are right words."*

Right words possess a life-giving force. They have the power to build, bless, and do good. This force of faith comes from Heaven and God Himself, transmitted through words. With good, positive words from God, we can strengthen people, businesses, families, relationships, and even our physical and mental health. On the other hand, words from the kingdom of darkness hinder progress—both our own and that of others.

That's why this book focuses on the power of words. My heart's desire is to see you succeed. My heart's desire is to see you empowered. My heart's desire is to see you live a victorious life—to see your family and future blessed through the power of God's love and His Word—His faith-filled words!

Romans 10:17 states, *"Faith comes by hearing, and hearing by the Word of God."*

Hebrews 11:1 adds, *"Through faith we understand that the worlds were framed by the Word of God, so that things which are seen were not made of things which do appear."*

These scriptures illustrate that faith is nurtured by hearing the Word of God. God's Word holds the unseen essence of faith. Wallace D. Wattles, in his book *The Science of Getting Rich*, discussed an unseen substance that fills all interspaces of the universe. He proposed that a thought within this substance can manifest into reality. Basically, a thought impressed on and into this substance creates and brings into existence the very thing thought about. I believe the unseen substance Wattles described is faith.

The scriptures reveals that God created the worlds through faith. They explain how creation came to be and how we can also access this invisible foundation—the unseen substance of all creation: faith. God has clearly shown us that faith is developed by consistently hearing His Word, not just once.

As believers, we must continually engage with the Word of God. We need to fill our hearts, minds, and mouths with the promises found in Scripture.

Jesus said in Matthew 4:4, *"Man shall not live on bread alone, but by every word that proceeds from the mouth of God."*

By meditating on, reading, and speaking God's Word, we nourish our inner man with faith. We strengthen our spirit with the fundamental element of the universe. As Hebrews 11:1 explains, the worlds were created by the Word of God, and we, too, can shape our world with His Word. In fact, it is crucial to use God's Word to frame our world if we wish to see His promises and blessings come to life.

You can apply the Word of God to your family, business, marriage, health, finances, future, and children—every aspect of your life. Speak the Word over your situations and trust it in your heart. Have faith that your words will become reality. Jesus Himself assured us of this.

In Mark 11:22–23, Jesus says, *"Have faith in God. For truly I say unto you, that whoever shall say to this mountain, 'Be removed, and be cast into the sea,' and shall not doubt in his heart, but shall believe that those things which he says shall come to pass; he shall have whatever he says."*

Here, Jesus teaches us to have the faith of God and to act on that faith by speaking to the mountains in our lives, commanding them to be removed. The ocean is the only place where a mountain can be buried and never seen again. That is the power God has given us to handle life's challenges.

Notice that in the above scripture, Jesus emphasises speaking three times and believing only once. This highlights the significance of confessing the desired outcome. We believe in our hearts and speak with our mouths what the Word declares. This is known as the confession of faith. Hebrews 10:23 states, *"Let us hold fast the confession of our faith without wavering; for he is faithful that promised."*

In Hebrews, we are encouraged to hold firmly to our confession of faith because the One who promised is faithful and will fulfil His Word. My wife once wisely said, *"Confess it and speak it until you believe it. Then confess it and speak it because you believe it!"*

This statement struck a chord with me—it was a moment of clarity. While believing in our hearts is essential, declaring and affirming our beliefs is equally important.

Mark 11:24 further emphasises this, stating, *"Therefore I say to you, whatever things you desire, when you pray, believe that you receive them, and you shall have them."*

Here, Jesus reassures us that whatever we desire in prayer, if we truly believe in our hearts that we have received it, the moment we prayed, then we shall have it. This is closely linked to the state of our hearts. The Word of God likens our hearts to soil. Just as soil yields a harvest from the seeds planted in it, our hearts yield a harvest from the words and thoughts planted in them.

Luke 6:45 explains, *"A good man out of the good treasure of his heart brings forth that which is good; and an evil man out of the evil treasure of his heart brings forth that which is evil: for out of the abundance of the heart his mouth speaks."*

Matthew 12:34 echoes this, saying, *"O generation of vipers, how can you, being evil, speak good things? For out of the abundance of the heart the mouth speaks."*

The harvest we gather depends on two factors: first, the seed we plant, and second, the ground into which we plant it.

Seed is created by God to reproduce itself, and the ground is designed to nurture and grow the seed that is planted. If you prepare the soil in your backyard, you can plant seeds for tomatoes or poison ivy. The ground will yield a crop based on the seed you plant. From the poison ivy seed, you will get poison ivy. From the tomato seed, you will get tomatoes. The ground does not decide what is planted —it is the sower, or the farmer, who makes that choice. The ground simply grows and produces what is planted. You decide what seeds—or words—you are planting into the ground of your heart and life today. You do this through the words you choose to speak. In Galatians 6:7, it states, *"Be not deceived; God is not mocked: for whatever a man sows, that shall he also reap."*

The Word of God teaches that as we sow, so shall we reap! You can plant harmful seeds in your heart, or you can plant good ones. The choice is yours. Remember the scripture we read earlier: Jesus said that out of the abundance of the heart, the mouth speaks! Another key factor is the heart. The Word of God compares our heart to ground, and for the ground to produce a bountiful harvest, it must be prepared—especially for good fruit. Have you noticed that weeds grow everywhere? Weeds even appear in the toughest and poorest of soils. However, when farmers want to produce a bountiful, good crop, they carefully prepare their soil, water it, and keep it fertilised until the harvest. They protect it from birds, fence out animals that might eat their crop, and remove weeds that would strangle it.

Now, let us apply this to our heart and the words we believe and speak that bring life and blessings. Jesus emphasised the importance of forgiveness when you stand praying and ask God for His blessings to manifest in your life. He highlighted this in Mark 11:25-26:

"And when you stand praying, forgive, if you have anything against anyone: that your Father also which is in heaven may forgive you your trespasses. But if you do not forgive, neither will your Father which is in heaven forgive your trespasses."

Jesus teaches us that His Word thrives best in a heart filled with love and forgiveness. When we forgive those who have wronged us, we channel God's love towards them. By seeking God's strength to forgive, we allow His divine nature to flow through us to others. This prepares our hearts to be fertile and sweet, enabling God's Word to grow within us.

Remember, what we sow is what will grow.

Galatians 6:8 reminds us, *"For he that sows to his flesh shall of the flesh reap corruption; but he that sows to the Spirit shall of the Spirit reap life everlasting."*

Through the Holy Spirit, the apostle Paul teaches us that we can either sow to our old flesh nature or to our new spirit man. In 2 Corinthians 5:17, it says, *"Therefore if any man be in Christ, he is a new creature: old things are passed away; behold, all things are become new."*

The Bible tells us that when someone is in Christ, they are born again as a new creation. Our new, born-again spirit is fertile ground, capable of producing the best results from the seeds sown into it. It is up to us what we sow, and we should only sow the seeds of the fruit we wish to harvest.

Holding onto unforgiveness or bitterness sours our hearts. Seeds sown into such ground will not yield the God-determined results they were meant to produce. Genesis 1:12 says, *"And the earth brought forth grass, and herb yielding seed after his kind, and the tree yielding fruit, whose seed was in itself, after his kind: and God saw that it was good."*

Every seed produces fruit after its kind, and God calls this good. This is how God designed the Earth to work, and He also designed our hearts and spirits to function in the same way.

God made man in His image (Genesis 1:26-27), empowering us to operate His system as He did. God blessed man by speaking over him—the same power He used to bring life into existence. From the beginning of creation, God gave people the power and authority to speak life, contained within the spoken blessing or the spoken Word.

The Parable of the Sower

In Mark 4:2-9, it says:

"And he taught them many things by parables, and said to them in his doctrine, Hearken; Behold, there went out a sower to sow: And it came to pass, as he sowed, some fell by the way side, and the fowls of

the air came and devoured it up. And some fell on stony ground, where it had not much earth; and immediately it sprang up, because it had no depth of earth: But when the sun was up, it was scorched; and because it had no root, it withered away. And some fell among thorns, and the thorns grew up, and choked it, and it yielded no fruit. And other fell on good ground, and did yield fruit that sprang up and increased; and brought forth, some thirty, and some sixty, and some an hundred. And he said to them, He that has ears to hear, let him hear."

Jesus Explains The Purpose Of Parables

In Mark 4:10-12 it says, "*And when he was alone, they that were about him with the twelve asked of him the parable. And he said to them, to you it is given to know the mystery of the kingdom of God: but to them that are without, all these things are done in parables: That seeing they may see, and not perceive; and hearing they may hear, and not understand; lest at any time they should be converted, and their sins should be forgiven them.*"

Jesus Made A Significant Statement When He Explained The Parable

In Mark 4:13-20 the Word says,*"And he said to them, Know you not this parable? and how then will you know all parables? The sower sows the word. And these are they by the way side, where the word is sown; but when they have heard, Satan comes immediately, and takes away the word that was sown in their hearts. And these are they likewise which are sown on stony ground; who, when they have heard the word, immediately receive it with gladness; And have no root in themselves, and so endure but for a time: afterward, when affliction or persecution arises for the word's sake, immediately they are offended. And these are they which are sown among thorns; such as hear the word, And the cares of this world, and the deceitfulness of riches, and the lusts of other things entering in, choke the word, and it becomes unfruitful. And these are they which are sown on good ground; such as hear the word, and receive it, and bring forth fruit, some thirtyfold, some sixty, and some an hundred."*

This is a powerful message! Jesus emphasised to His disciples that grasping this parable is essential for understanding all parables. Without understanding how this parable functions, one cannot comprehend the workings of the Kingdom of God. However, with the guidance of the Holy Spirit, you can gain insight and revelation into this parable. The seed represents the Word of God, and within the seed lies the life of God!

The Bible tells us that the love of money is the root of all evil, not money itself. Money is a tool, a resource to give and share. God actually wants you to be blessed, so you can be a blessing! Satan's problem was that he wanted it all. He didn't want to share. Sharing is caring, God wants, desires and wishes for you to be blessed with increase. Then you can give, and help others. You can tithe to your local church, support the spreading of the gospel, help your family, the poor and needy, charitable causes, individuals, and just enjoy life in general.

This book aims to provide you with understanding, insight, and revelation knowledge about God's Word system and the incredible power of words. Once you grasp this, you can begin to harness this power—available to everyone. You can release the power of words through your speech, with faith in your heart, to transform your circumstances and shape the future direction of your life. You can mould your world, future, and family with the Word of God.

The Secret Power Of The Tongue

Chapter Four:

Dominion

"And God said, Let us make man in our image, after our likeness: and let them have dominion over the fish of the sea, and over the fowl of the air, and over the cattle, and over all the earth, and over every creeping thing that creeps upon the earth."
— Genesis 1:26.

God declared that man was to have dominion over all creation (Genesis 1:26), including the fish of the sea, the birds of the air, the cattle, all the earth, and every creeping creature. He entrusted and imparted this dominion to them by speaking *"The Blessing"* over them.

But how was man to exercise this dominion over God's creation? In the same way God did— with words! God created the Earth for man, not for Himself or the devil, He made it for us that we might have dominion over it. God made the Earth for us! He made us for Himself! I like to say, *"God made the universe for the Earth, the Earth for people, and people for Himself!"* God desired a family. He wants you to be His unique son or precious daughter and to be your father. God loves you, wants to be your father, and desires you to be blessed with the same blessing He gave Abraham, *"The Blessing of the Lord,"* also known as the Abraham Covenant Blessing.

God Is A Faith God

To bring the world into existence, God had to use His faith. Hebrews 11:3 reveals, *"Through faith we understand that the worlds were framed by the Word of God."* In the beginning, when God spoke, He believed with all His heart that what He said with His mouth was going to come to pass. His spoken word then became reality. When He commanded, *"Let there be light!"* Light was! This pattern continued as God manifested what He believed and declared, with His mouth.

As He spoke with faith, the universe came together, and the worlds were created by the Word of God.

Hebrews 11:1 describes faith as, *"the substance of things hoped for, the evidence of things not seen."*

In his book, *The Science of Getting Rich*, Wallace D. Wattles says, *"There is a thinking substance from which all things are made, and which in its original state, permeates and fills all the interspaces of the universe. A thought within this substance produces the thing that is imagined by the thought."* It brings it into being.

A person can form things in their thoughts, their imagination, and by pressing their thought upon the formless substance, can cause the thing they think about to be created. Wattles says, do not ask why these things are true, nor speculate as how they can be true. Simply take them on trust.

I submit to you, he was talking about faith. We need to take God at His Word, believe it, trust it, meditate it, and release it by speaking words. We need to rely on Him, by having faith and confidence in His Word. If God said it, then it is so!

Doctors often say we are what we eat. I agree, as this holds true in both physical and spiritual realms. What we meditate on, what we perceive, and what we allow to enter into our spirit will eventually manifest through our words. We must agree with God's declarations about who we are and reject the devil's attempts to sway us off God's Word. The devil is always trying to tell us: *"You're a no good, sinner! A failure! And you're unworthy."*

Romans 3:3-4 asserts: *"For what if some did not believe? Shall their unbelief make the faith of God without effect? God forbid: yes, let God be true, but every man a liar; as it is written, That you might be justified in your sayings, and might overcome when you are judged."*

Remember, God is a Creator, and we were made in His image and likeness. As mini creators, we are destined to manifest His goodness and blessings on Earth. God desires for us to have dominion in our sphere of influence and to achieve victory in every area of our life.

The word *"dominion"* embodies supreme authority or sovereignty, encompassing control over the natural world. It signifies the ruler of a region and his authority over it, with the area often named after the ruler's dominion. Dominion means to dominate, rule, and reign. We were created by God to have dominion over this Earth, both in the natural and supernatural realms, or what we can call the realm of the spirit.

In Genesis 1:28, the Bible states, *"And God blessed them, and God said to them, Be fruitful, and multiply, and replenish the earth, and subdue it: and have dominion over the fish of the sea, and over the fowl of the air, and over every living thing that moves upon the earth."*

Notice the two words here, *"subdue"* and *"dominion."* These are intriguing Hebrew words. *"Subdue"* is the Hebrew word *"Kabash,"* pronounced *Kah-vash*, meaning to subdue, subject, force, keep under, or bring into subjection. It implies conquering and bringing under control, as seen in the act of subduing the Earth or enemies. This indicates a sense of stewardship or dominion granted by God, reflecting His divine mandate to govern creation. Adam and Eve, along with their future descendants, were to govern creation and subdue their enemies—those of God and the Earth, both natural and spiritual. The use of *"Kabash"* in the Hebrew Bible reflects the cultural understanding of authority and responsibility.

The Hebrew word *"dominion"* here is *"radah,"* pronounced *rah-DAH* (raw-daw). According to Strong's Concordance, it means to rule, have dominion, subdue, and tread down. In the Hebrew context, *"dominion"* primarily refers to ruling or having authority over something. It suggests exercising control, often in governance or stewardship.

In the Biblical story, *"radah"* is frequently used to describe humanity's authority over creation and the rule of kings and leaders over their subjects. Rulers were viewed as stewards of God, responsible for maintaining order and justice. The Biblical use of *"radah"* reflects this understanding, emphasising responsibility and benevolent leadership. In Genesis, the idea of dominion is not about exploitation but about stewardship and care of God's creation. Humanity was to bless it, protect it, increase it, and enjoy it, exercising this authority through words spoken in faith and under God's ultimate authority.

We have a powerful revelation here: God was warning Adam and Eve about enemies that needed to be subdued. Even in Eden, paradise, they had to steward, protect, increase, and bring under control any enemies that threatened this utopia. God had planted the Garden of Eden on Earth and placed Adam and Eve there. This fertile, rich paradise was to be governed by Adam and Eve under God's ultimate authority, and they were to *"Edenise"* the Earth. In other words, they were to expand Eden to cover the entire Earth. How? Using *"The Blessing,"* through the spoken word and the seeds God provided.

God was revealing to people the presence of an enemy, not one to be feared, but one to be dominated, controlled, and brought under subjection. This enemy was the fallen angel Lucifer, now known as Satan. Satan had rebelled against God and His Word, His rule, and divine law, causing him to fall from Heaven. He became the arch-enemy of God and all His creation.

In John 10:10, Jesus warned us, *"The thief comes not, but for to steal, and to kill, and to destroy: I am come that they might have life, and that they might have it more abundantly."*

Satan became the ruler of darkness and all the disobedient spirits from the pre-Adamic creation. God was warning Adam and Eve, and their future descendants, that they would need to subdue and dominate this being, their enemies, and the forces of darkness in this world.

This authority and dominion were to be expressed and exercised through words—words of spirit and life. God's Word—God's faith-filled Word. Jesus said in Luke 10:18, *"I beheld Satan as lightning fall from heaven."*

Satan was cast out of Heaven and brought down to Earth. Now, humanity is not to fear him but rather to subdue, control, and have dominion over him.

Where the first man, Adam, failed, the second man, the second Adam, succeeded! Jesus Christ defeated Satan and the powers of darkness in this world, along with all the fallen angels and principalities and powers in Heavenly places. He has now given us His authority, the power of attorney, and the right to speak in His name, enabling us to cast out, pull down, and bind principalities and powers.

Luke 10:19 states, *"Behold, I give unto you power to tread on serpents and scorpions, and over all the power of the enemy: and nothing shall by any means hurt you."*

God's people are to do this through words—words of faith, words from God's Word, spoken by your tongue over the circumstances or enemy attacking. Again, people are to release the blessing over creation and have dominion. Galatians 3:29 says, *"And if you be Christ's, then are you Abraham's seed, and heirs according to the promise."*

We are to speak this blessing in faith, believing that what we say with our mouth will come to pass—and it will come to pass in time! Because there is a seed time and a harvest time! And the Word says, *"by faith and patience we inherit the promises"* (Hebrews 6:12).

Where the first Adam failed, let us succeed through Jesus Christ and His spoken Word. You were called to win in life through Jesus Christ. As the seed of Abraham, we are to operate the same blessing given to Adam and Eve in the Garden of Eden, bringing and releasing God's Kingdom on Earth. God has empowered you to win, and you do it through words—spoken with your mouth and believed in your heart.

As Christians, we must ensure that when it comes to spiritual matters, we are not like those potato men we played with as kids. Potato men have big heads because they think they know everything, and the Word of God warns us that knowledge puffs people up. Instead, we must remain humble before God, open to correction, and have a teachable spirit. We should keep our ears open to what the Spirit of God wants to say and our eyes open to see how God wants to use us in the future. God has big plans and dreams for our lives. Jeremiah 29:11 reminds us:

"For I know the thoughts that I think toward you, says the Lord, thoughts of peace, and not of evil, to give you an expected end."

God wants to give you a future filled with great hope, where your desires and dreams are fulfilled!

Remember, "you have authority." And authority is the right to determine the outcome of circumstances and events.

The Secret Power Of The Tongue

Chapter Five:

Imitate God

"Therefore be imitators of God as dear children."
— **Ephesians 5:1**

Now that we are born-again and open to learning like God's little children, we must understand how Jesus operated within His Father's Word system. As James 1:22 instructs, we should be doers of the Word, not just hearers. We should follow Jesus' example, walking in His way, truth, and life.

God expects us to function in the same manner as He does through His Word system. By speaking out His Word in faith, we can witness the circumstances surrounding us, those that stand in our way, transform and fall before us as we engage with God's Word system. In the unseen realm, spiritual forces, both angelic and demonic, principalities and powers, are at work. Our words empower both the good and evil forces. Scripture, in Psalm 103:19-22, shows that angels, mightily excel in strength in carrying out God's commands, by obeying the voice of His Word. We give voice to the Word with our tongue, as we speak His Word.

"The Lord has established His throne in heaven, And His kingdom rules over all. Bless the Lord, you His angels, Who excel in strength, who do His Word, listening to the voice of His Word. Bless the Lord, all you His hosts, You ministers of His, who do His pleasure. Bless the Lord, all His works, In all places of His dominion. Bless the Lord, O my soul!"

The Word or manna from Heaven fed angels! Jesus is the true manna who came down from Heaven and His Word now feeds our soul and spirit.

This shows why it's crucial for us to learn to speak the positive, good, and faith-filled Word of God. Our words either work for us or against us by empowering good or evil forces in the spirit realm.

We should empower the angels God has sent to protect us by speaking His Word and commands into the atmosphere around our lives, families, and homes. Focus on speaking what you want, not what you don't want. My good friend Don Gossett, who wrote many books on words and the power of the tongue, co-authored a book with E.W. Kenyan. He shared with me that God spoke to him, saying, *"My people are saying what they have, when they should be having what they say."*

This gave Don insight into the power of our words and the tongue. This revelation was so profound in

Don's life that he dedicated his lifetime to studying the empowerment of words spoken by believers. God wants believers to have what they say, what they confess. He doesn't want His children or believers constantly speaking curses or circumstances in their lives.

In other words, God doesn't want His children constantly speaking negative words that only reinforce the curse and empower fallen, demonic forces. Remember, God is working behind the scenes to bless you. He has sent forth His angels to work, minister, and advocate for you. That work is reinforced by you speaking the blessing or promised benefit in His Word.

When Jesus taught us to pray, *"God's Kingdom come,"* He was encouraging us to pray for God's way of doing things and His method of operation to return to Earth. God desires for you to experience Heaven on Earth!

Deuteronomy 11:21 says: *"That your days may be multiplied, and the days of your children, in the land which the LORD swore unto your fathers to give them, as the days of heaven upon the earth."*

Hebrews 11:6 reminds us, *"but without faith it is impossible to please Him: for he that comes to God must believe that He is (God is) and that He is a rewarder of them that diligently seek Him."*

Jesus also encouraged us to have the faith of God, as mentioned in Mark 11:22-26:

"And Jesus answering says to them, Have the faith of God. For verily I say to you, That whoever shall say to this mountain, Be you removed, and be you cast into the sea; and shall not doubt in his heart, but shall believe that those things which he says shall come to pass; he shall have whatever he says. Therefore I say to you, Whatever things you desire, when you pray, believe that you receive them, and you shall have them. And when you stand praying, forgive, if you have anything against anyone: that your Father also which is in heaven may forgive you your trespasses. But if you do not forgive, neither will your Father which is in heaven forgive your trespasses."

As we read over the above passages, Jesus was giving us an example and urging us to operate the same way God operates. Jesus is teaching us, if we are going to move mountains then we need to operate according to His example.

Right from the start, from the Garden of Eden, the spoken Word was the effective way to bring blessings. When people engaged with with the Word, it brought life, by speaking it forth with belief, conviction, and boldness. The first man, Adam, understood this principle and operated within God's Word system.

Adam Operated Within God's Word System

Consider what Adam says in Genesis 2:23-24 *"This is now bone of my bones, and flesh of my flesh: she shall be called woman, because she was taken out of man. Therefore shall a man leave his father and his mother, and cleave unto his wife: and they shall be one flesh."*

To this day, we still refer to a lady as a woman. In fact, Adam named Eve *"woman."*

Adam prophesied the ordination of marriage. The words he spoke over the institution of marriage have endured to this day. Jesus referred to it in the first two gospels, and Paul discussed it in the epistles.

In Genesis 2:18-19, God allowed man to name His creation because He had given him dominion over all things on Earth. Adam, Eve, and their future descendants were given dominion by God over all creation. God imparted this dominion and authority to Adam through His spoken Word in Genesis 1:26-28, where He said:

"And God said, Let us make man in our image, after our likeness: and let them have dominion over the fish of the sea, and over the fowl of the air, and

over the cattle, and over all the earth, and over every creeping thing that creeps upon the earth. So God created man in his own image, in the image of God created he him; male and female created he them. And God blessed them, and God said to them, Be fruitful, and multiply, and replenish the earth, and subdue it: and have dominion over the fish of the sea, and over the fowl of the air, and over every living thing that moves upon the earth."

In verse 28, we see that God blessed them by speaking His blessing of increase over them. From this verse, we can see how God was demonstrating and showing man how to operate. God was commanding man to operate, in the same way He Himself exercised authority and dominion over the entirety of creation. Adam and Eve and their future seed were to operate and exercise their authority in the same way God did.

Chapter Six:

Jesus Operated This Way!

"For I have not spoken of myself; but the Father which sent me, he gave me a commandment, what I should say, and what I should speak."
— John 12:49

Jesus operated in this way! He also used God's Word system, which God had given to people from the beginning. Jesus did not defeat the devil as God, but rather as a man under the blessing of Abraham, fulfilling the old covenant law completely, and obeying God by doing what God had shown people to do. He operated The Blessing by speaking and proclaiming the Word!

Let's read Matthew 4:1-10:

"Then Jesus was led by the Spirit into the wilderness to be tempted by the devil. After fasting for forty days and forty nights, he was hungry. When the tempter came to him, he said, "If you are the Son of God, command these stones to become bread." But Jesus replied, "It is written: Man shall not live on bread alone, but on every word that comes from the

mouth of God." Then the devil took him up to the holy city and set him on the pinnacle of the temple. He said to him, "If you are the Son of God, throw yourself down. For it is written: He will give his angels charge concerning you, and they will bear you up on their hands, so that you may not strike your foot against a stone." Jesus said to him, "It is written again: You shall not tempt the Lord your God." Again, the devil took him up to an exceedingly high mountain and showed him all the kingdoms of the world and their glory. He said to him, "All these things I will give you if you will fall down and worship me." Then Jesus said to him, "Go away, Satan! For it is written: You shall worship the Lord your God, and him only shall you serve."

In this passage, notice how Jesus resisted temptation and the devil. Jesus declared that man was to live by every word that comes from the mouth of God! What did Jesus do? He stood firm on the Word! He resisted Satan with the Word of God.

Jesus lived by the Word and conquered the devil through the words He spoke. This is God's way of bringing the Kingdom to Earth, through the spoken blessing.

When the disciples asked Jesus to teach them to pray, He began with the Lord's Prayer, asking them to pray for God's kingdom to come on Earth as it is in Heaven (Matthew 6:10).

God's method is here! We can overcome temptation, the evil one, and all his attacks by speaking God's Word and promises against the circumstances that oppose us. Let's read the next scripture from this passage.

Matthew 4:11 says, *"Then the devil left him, and, behold, angels came and ministered unto him."*

This scripture clearly teaches us how powerful God's Word is when applied to life. In verse 4, we learn that people need not only physical food but also spiritual food, found in God's written Word, the Bible, to live a strong life both physically and spiritually. Jesus then reveals how He uses the written and spoken Word of God to defeat the devil during their spiritual battle. From verse 11, we see that after this encounter with Satan and the forces of darkness, through using God's Word, Satan was forced to leave, and angels came to minister to Jesus. This passage beautifully illustrates how the spoken Word repels darkness and empowers good angels to come and serve us.

I like to say that, when we speak the Word of God, whether it's the written Word or the promises revealed to us through scripture, or when we pray in the Holy

Spirit, we are giving commands to the angels. By speaking God's Word in faith or praying in the gift of tongues, as led by the Holy Spirit, you are indeed giving commands to the angels of God. These angels are incredibly strong and carry out God's Word, always listening and ready to act.

The Apostle Paul Operated In This Manner

2 Corinthians 4:13 states, *"We having the same spirit of faith, according as it is written, I believed, and therefore have I spoken; we also believe, and therefore speak;"*

In the Bible, Paul urged the Church to follow his example as he followed Christ's (1 Corinthians 4:16 & 1 Corinthians 11:1).

In Romans 1:16-17, Paul declares: *"For I am not ashamed of the gospel of Christ: for it is the power of God to salvation to every one that believes; to the Jew first, and also to the Greek. For there is the righteousness of God revealed from faith to faith: as it is written, The just shall live by faith."*

John 1:1,14 tells us, *"In the beginning was the Word, and the Word was with God and the Word was God...And the Word became flesh and dwelt among us."*

You and I can work together to create a better life and future for ourselves and our families. We are made in the likeness of God and redeemed by the precious blood of Jesus Christ from our old sin nature. We are also given the free gift of righteousness through Jesus' blood when He died for us on the cross of Calvary.

As it is written, *"The first man Adam was made a living soul; the last Adam was made a life-giving Spirit."* (1 Corinthians 15:45)

Words have the power to create, shape, and change things! This is why I teach about confessing the Word, the power of the tongue, the authority of the Word, and the impact of the Word in your mouth when spoken in faith.

It's not mind over matter, but a divine system established by God. This is how we are meant to operate on Earth.

I like to say, "It's God's mind (His Word) over everything that matters to our lives!"

It's a spiritual law set by God when He created this realm. By filling our hearts with God's Word and speaking them in faith, we can change our circumstances, our position in life, and overcome the evil one through, *"the blood of the lamb and the word of our testimony!"* (Revelation 12:11) This is our responsibility. We all have this sacred trust and divine right. We owe it to our future selves, our families and the generations to come, to speak right.

Life Talk

I call this your life talk! God has given each of us a voice. You have a voice! And He wants you to use it to speak the right words. Words of faith should continually flow from your heart through your mouth to see your world change for the better.

Job 6:25A says, *"How forcible are right words!"*

Proverbs 18:21 says, *"Death and life are in the power of the tongue and they that love it, we eat the fruit thereof."*

Choose words of life that you and your seed may live!

Jesus said in Matthew 12:24, *"Out of the abundance of the heart the mouth speaks!"*

Jesus Operated This Way!

We are to speak God's Word from our mouths as it comes from our hearts.

In Mark 4, the parable of the sower, Jesus explained how the Word enters the heart of man. From there, it starts to grow and produce life after its own kind. Jesus said, we can produce from that seed 30, 60, and up to 100-fold increase. God is looking for us to produce fruits. He wants us to produce His life in us. When we give or invest in the natural, we look for a harvest, we look for an increase on our investment.

We invest our time, our money, and our life into different things, expecting to get something back. We desire an increase on our investment.

God is not different, He is looking for an increase on His investment into your life and future. We are born-again, our hearts are being renewed by His Spirit, through His Word (His Son). Now He wants us to plant His Word into our hearts and speak it with our mouth to reproduce His life in us. So we can bring forth fruit for His glory; multiplying it 30, 60, and up to a 100 times.

God actually gets upset with believers that waste His talents and abilities, that He has placed within them. He wants you to use what you have to gain more, to increase and expand His Kingdom of Earth.

We can do this, by becoming doers of the Word, not hearers only. We need to put into practise in our lives the principles found in His Word. As we do this, we will be blessed in the doing.

Chapter Seven:

Sow the Word

"While the earth remains, Seedtime and harvest, Cold and heat, Winter and summer, And day and night Shall not cease."
— Genesis 8:22

    God's Word must be planted in your heart, which He designed to yield what is sown. However, the seed is not truly planted until you comprehend it. This is why Proverbs 3:13 advises seeking wisdom and understanding. To grasp the wisdom from the Word, we must learn to apply it to our lives. If we ask the Holy Spirit for understanding, He will grant us insight into all aspects of life and godliness. Wisdom is the ability to use knowledge. God assures us, through His Holy Spirit, as we pursue Him in His Word and nourish ourselves with it daily, He will cultivate in our hearts and lives knowledge, wisdom, and understanding.

The words you hear and speak most frequently are the ones your heart will most likely believe.

The Word is the seed! Your heart is the soil! This is why Jesus advised us to be mindful of what we hear (Luke 8:18). What enters our ears will settle in our hearts. The words you hear and speak most frequently are the ones your heart will most likely believe. Your words can either benefit or harm you; it's your choice. God's Words will cultivate faith in your heart. When you speak them out in faith, they will manifest in your life and bring blessings.

Jesus also exhorted us to operate this way!

Jesus not only lived by God's Word system but also encouraged us to follow suit. As the Good Teacher, He is the key to life, joy, freedom, wealth, and prosperity—everything that brings happiness, fulfilment, and goodness, both in this life and in eternity. He shared His teachings so we can embrace the victory He won for us on the cross through His sacrifice. Success is a journey, not just a destination. Jesus wants to empower you to thrive by integrating God's laws and principles into your life.

Recognising the power of words and the influence of your tongue is one of the most vital lessons you'll ever learn, as it shapes your entire existence.

In James 3:4-9 we read:

"Behold also the ships, which though they be so great, and are driven of fierce winds, yet are they turned about with a very small helm, wherever the governor lists. Even so the tongue is a little member, and boasts great things. Behold, how great a matter a little fire kindles! And the tongue is a fire, a world of iniquity: so is the tongue among our members, that it defiles the whole body, and sets on fire the course of nature; and it is set on fire of hell. For every kind of beasts, and of birds, and of serpents, and of things in the sea, is tamed, and has been tamed of mankind: But the tongue can no man tame; it is an unruly evil,

full of deadly poison. Therefore bless we God, even the Father; and therewith curse we men, which are made after the similitude of God."

The book of James illustrates that massive ocean ships are guided by a small rudder, which the captain turns to set the ship's course. In the same way, although our tongue is tiny, it influences the entire direction of our life. Speaking negatively can lead to fear and anxiety. Whatever you say will yield results in your life. Your heart will most likely believe the words you speak.

Proverbs 23:7 reminds us, *"for as he thinks in his heart, so is he."*

Your beliefs and words have the power to shape your reality. What you speak will eventually come to fruition.

Think of it this way: your word is like a seed. An apple seed grows into an apple tree that produces apples— full of seeds! And a thorn seed produces thorns. As Genesis 1:11 teaches, every seed bears fruit true to its nature: *"And God said, Let the earth bring forth grass, the herb yielding seed, and the fruit tree yielding fruit after his kind, whose seed is in itself, upon the earth: and it was so."*

Imagine your heart as a fertile field, ready to nurture the seeds of your thoughts. When you plant these seeds and water them with faith, emotions, or even fear, they blossom into the fruits of your decisions. The harvest you gather is a direct reflection of what you've sown. If your current results aren't to your liking, it's time to shift your focus and plant something new.

It's Your Choice

Deuteronomy 30:19 states, *"I call heaven and earth to witness against you today, that I have set before you life and death, blessing and cursing. Therefore, choose life, that you and your descendants may live."*

You choose life by tuning into God's Word, the seed of wisdom, and allowing it take root deeply in your heart, the fertile soil of your soul. Then, with unwavering faith, you voice it out, nurturing it as it blossoms into a mighty tree. This tree, in its full glory, bears abundant fruit, a nourishing feast that sustains you on your journey through life.

Genesis 8:22 proclaims, *"While the earth remains, seedtime and harvest, and cold and heat, and summer and winter, and day and night shall not cease."*

Imagine the thrill of planting a seed, the anticipation of watching it grow with tender care, and the joy of finally harvesting its rich bounty! This is the vibrant cycle of life, the life of a seed, full of promise and potential.

There is a planting time, and there is a growing time. During this time we need to keep it (the thing desired) well watered. We need to pull out the weeds (negative thoughts and doubts) reinforcing the vision, the dream, or the thing desired with positive food. That is, confessions of faith and praise that lead to the manifestation of what we are believing for and calling into being. There is a seed time and a harvest time!

Chapter Eight:

What You See In Your Mind, Comes To Pass In Time

"Let us hold fast the profession of our faith without wavering; (for he is faithful that promised;)."
— **Hebrews 10:23**

What you see in your mind comes to pass in time. Create vibrant, positive pictures in your mind of what you're dreaming of achieving. Imagine yourself healed, performing tasks that once seemed impossible, or engaging in activities that bring you immense joy. Let these images dance in your mind's eye, infuse your thought-life, and ignite your imagination. Visualise yourself in perfect health, and then affirm it with your words! Fill your heart and mind with uplifting scripture, the promises from God's Word that assure you of healing or whatever you're believing for. Meditate on these promises by creating mental images of yourself thriving and whole.

This principle applies to all your aspirations, whether it's financial abundance, a fulfilling relationship, a new career, a business venture, personal development, a fitter and healthier you, crypto going to the moon, a dream home, a motorbike, a push-bike, a majestic boat, a successful, growing ministry or winning your family to Jesus etc. Whatever captures your heart's desire, seek out promises in God's Word and weave them into the fabric of your dreams and visions.

You need to write the vision. As the Bible says in Habakkuk 2:2, *"And the LORD answered me, and said, Write the vision, and make it plain upon tables, that he may run that reads it."*

Imagine the life you're dreaming of and capture it in vibrant pictures! Display these images prominently where you can see them every day, and let them inspire your journey. Frame them with powerful words from God's Word, and jot down scriptures that assure you of His promise. I love to say, *"Seed the vision, or the dream, with the Word of God!"* Just like you nurture seeds in the soil, think about planting a financial seed in the Kingdom of God, your local church, or a thriving ministry. Give that seed a purpose, or an assignment, by naming the abundant harvest you anticipate.

Years back, I had a dream of owning a Jet Ski. Whenever my kids were little, we'd stroll through shopping centres, eyes drawn to the sleek, shiny Jet

What You See In Your Mind Comes To Pass In Time

Skis displayed as art union prizes. I'd excitedly tell them, *"I'm believing for a Jet Ski!"* and thank God that I already had one, even though it was way out of our budget.

I'd often head to the beach, standing in awe as people zoomed across the waves on their Jet Skis. Watching them glide up and down the water, I'd raise my hands in praise, feeling the thrill of owning one myself. I'd vividly picture myself out on the water, leaping over waves, and giving my kids the ride of their lives on the back.

During our family holidays, I saved up enough to hire a Jet Ski a couple of times. Those moments were unforgettable, filled with the exhilaration of riding for the first time and the joy of sharing it with my young children.

For years, I held onto the belief that I owned a Jet Ski, sharing vivid tales of our adventures with my wife. These stories were filled with positive emotions and excitement, as I imagined myself soaring over waves on a hired Jet Ski. Despite the years passing, I never let go of this dream.

Then, one day, a family friend of my son, who was a passionate and meticulous Jet Ski rider, decided to upgrade to a faster, bigger model. He offered me an incredible deal on his second-hand Jet Ski. I vividly remember picking it up and bringing it home, feeling a sense of accomplishment.

The first family outing on our Jet Ski to the river mouth was unforgettable. We spent the day laughing and enjoying the thrill of the ride together. This blessing was just the beginning, as God continued to provide for us financially. A couple of years later, I was able to trade in our Jet Ski for a brand-new, top-of-the-range three-seater model!

This new Jet Ski brought countless hours of joy and adventure to our family. It all started with a dream, a promise, and a seed planted in God's kingdom. With faith and the power of my words, I nurtured that seed, and the vision I held dear became a reality. The dream I spoke of manifested, bringing us closer together and creating cherished memories.

Meet Stuart Ballantyne, a remarkable businessman and a passionate church minister whose life is a testament to the power of words. Over the years, Stewart has captivated audiences with his inspiring messages, urging them to be mindful of their speech. His personal journey and ministry have revealed the incredible influence of the words we speak. Stewart is a firm believer in the power of positivity, and no matter how he feels, his response is always the same, *"I am fantastic and getting better."*

I've witnessed Stewart navigate life's ups and downs with unwavering optimism. His consistent positive affirmations have not only shaped his own life but have also inspired others. One such story is that of a friend who faced a life-threatening battle with cancer. Miraculously healed, this friend credits his recovery to Stewart's teachings on confessing God's Word over his health and future. Stewart encouraged him to respond to inquiries about his well-being with the same mantra, *"I am fantastic and getting better!"*

This teaching underscores a profound truth: your soul, spirit, mind, will, and emotions are more influenced by your own words than by anyone else's. God has crafted you to believe what you say about yourself. Your voice holds unparalleled authority and persuasiveness in your life. Therefore, it is vital to align your words with what God declares about you, shaping a future filled with hope and possibility.

Confession

In the Bible, the concept of confession carries a powerful positive meaning. It involves affirming what God has declared in His Word, serving as a witness to its truth. It's about testifying to the revelations found in the Bible and echoing God's perspective on any situation.

Hebrews 10:23 encourages us, *"Let us hold fast the confession of our faith without wavering (for he is faithful who promised)."* This verse reminds us of the importance of steadfastly clinging to our faith and the promises God has made.

Beyond just holding onto our confession, we are called to continually affirm the truths God has unveiled to us, ensuring that His word remains a vibrant part of our lives.

Titus 3:8-9 says: *"This is a faithful saying, and these things I will that you affirm constantly, that they which have believed in God might be careful to maintain good works. These things are good and profitable to men. But avoid foolish questions, and genealogies, and contentions, and strivings about the law; for they are unprofitable and vain."*

2 Peter 1:12 says, *"For this reason I will not be negligent to remind you always of these things, though you know and are established in the present truth."*

We must get established in this truth of confessing God's Word. There is breakthrough and victory in its application to our lives.

What You See In Your Mind Comes To Pass In Time

The Preacher's job is to teach. Ephesians 4:11-18 says:

"And he gave some, apostles; and some, prophets; and some, evangelists; and some, pastors and teachers; For the perfecting of the saints, for the work of the ministry, for the edifying of the body of Christ: Till we all come in the unity of the faith, and of the knowledge of the Son of God, unto a perfect man, unto the measure of the stature of the fulness of Christ: That we henceforth be no more children, tossed to and fro, and carried about with every wind of doctrine, by the sleight of men, and cunning craftiness, whereby they lie in wait to deceive; But speaking the truth in love, may grow up into him in all things, which is the head, even Christ: From whom the whole body fitly joined together and compacted by that which every joint supplies, according to the effectual working in the measure of every part, makes increase of the body unto the edifying of itself in love. This I say therefore, and testify in the Lord, that you henceforth walk not as other Gentiles walk, in the vanity of their mind, Having the understanding darkened, being alienated from the life of God through the ignorance that is in them, because of the blindness of their heart."

These verses highlight the profound impact of our learning and speech. Imagine God inviting us to a deeper understanding of faith and the knowledge of

His Son, Jesus Christ. The King James Version speaks of a *"perfect man,"* but the true essence is a mature individual. God desires us to mature into the full stature of Christ. Verse 15 reminds us to confess the truth in love, a powerful combination that draws us closer to God and His Son in every aspect.

In verse 16, we are reminded that as part of the body of Christ, we are all connected by the Spirit of God. Each of us has a unique role to play, contributing positive words of love, encouragement, and edification that nurture and uplift our spiritual family. Verses 17 and 18 urge us to avoid the futility of our minds, where ignorance can darken our understanding and separate us from God's life.

Many of us underestimate the power of our words, which can either build up or tear down those around us—our families, partners, spouses, workmates, church members, and communities. As we continue reading in Ephesians 4:22, the Bible calls us to abandon our corrupt and harmful past conversations. Verse 23 then speaks of renewal: *"That you put off concerning the former conversation the old man, which is corrupt according to the deceitful lusts; And be renewed in the spirit of your mind"*

Let's embrace this renewal and let our words be a beacon of love and truth. Our mind is made up of our will and emotions. Our thinking processes are in our mind. How we think, how we feel, how we see a situation or circumstance. Many times, how we see or feel a circumstance, can be affected by our previous conversations and life experiences.

God wants us renewed in the spirit of our mind! It says in Ephesians 4:25, *"therefore putting away lying, speak every man truth with his neighbour: for we are members one of another."*

God calls us to communicate the truth of His Word with our neighbours and friends. What does His Word reveal about our lives? Our health? Our future and hope? By sharing these insights, we can uplift, encourage, and strengthen our family, friends, and the community we cherish.

However, some of us may be unknowingly tearing down our homes, families, and relationships by echoing the negative words of circumstances instead of the positive promises of God. We can acknowledge these challenges without resorting to falsehoods. The key is to rise above them, denying them the power to dictate our lives. While we don't ignore their existence, we counteract them by speaking the life-giving Word of God, affirming His promises over our circumstances.

This is the essence of the Abraham kind of faith—the God kind of faith. As Romans 4:16-17 beautifully states, *"Therefore it is of faith, that it might be by grace; to the end the promise might be sure to all the seed; not to that only which is of the law, but to that also which is of the faith of Abraham; who is the father of us all, (As it is written, I have made thee a father of many nations,) before him whom he believed, even God, who makes alive the dead, and calls those things which be not as though they were."*

We can see that Abraham operated in the God kind of faith by calling those things that be not as though they were! Abraham operated the way God operated. Let's read Romans 4:18-22:

"Who against hope believed in hope, that he might become the father of many nations, according to that which was spoken, So shall your seed be. And being not weak in faith, he considered not his own body now dead, when he was about an hundred years old, neither yet the deadness of Sarah's womb: He staggered not at the promise of God through unbelief; but was strong in faith, giving glory to God; And being fully persuaded that, what he had promised, he was able also to perform. And therefore it was imputed to him for righteousness."

Imagine the scene: Abraham, nearly 100 years old, and Sarah, around 90, both far beyond child-bearing years. Yet, from verse 18, we witness Abraham's unwavering hope to become the father of many nations through his own son. Despite the natural impossibility, Abraham's faith was not shaken. The Bible describes his body as *"dead"* in that area, but he refused to let the circumstances dictate his belief. Instead, he clung to God's promise, fully convinced that what God had declared, He could and would fulfil.

Abraham's journey of faith is a powerful testament to the transformative power of belief. He didn't just believe; he glorified God with praise and thankfulness, turning on the tap of faith within himself. This conviction led to a change in his identity, as God renamed him from Abram, meaning *"exalted father,"* to Abraham, meaning *"father of a multitude."* Every time Sarah spoke to him, she was now calling him the father of many nations, and his servants echoed this new reality. Abraham embraced his new name, aligning his self-perception with God's Word, and called into existence what was not yet there.

His faith was so profound that God declared it righteousness. When we believe and speak the Word of God, we honour His integrity and the integrity of His Word. It's a form of worship to trust that what God says is true. Abraham's story is an inspiring reminder that with faith, all things are possible, and that belief is a work of righteousness that honours God. Romans 5:1-5 beautifully illustrates this:

"Therefore being justified by faith, we have peace with God through our Lord Jesus Christ: By whom also we have access by faith into this grace wherein we stand, and rejoice in hope of the glory of God. And not only so, but we glory in tribulations also: knowing that tribulation works patience; And patience, experience; and experience, hope: And hope makes not ashamed; because the love of God is shed abroad in our hearts by the Holy Ghost which is given to us."

This faith brings us peace with God through our Lord Jesus Christ, allowing us to stand in His grace and rejoice in the hope of His glory. Even in times of tribulation and trials, we find hope and confidence, knowing that by standing in grace and faith, we embrace God's promises. Patience emerges, leading to experience and hope, which ensures we are never ashamed. God's love, poured into our hearts by the Holy Spirit, is evident from the very beginning, as seen in Genesis 1, where the Holy Spirit hovered over the waters, ready to bring God's Word to life. The Father, the Word, and the Spirit work in perfect unity, manifesting God's will in our lives and on Earth. God's love is profound, demonstrated by sending His Son, Jesus Christ, to die for us while we were still sinners. Jesus' sacrifice freed us from sin, wrath, and judgment, transforming us from death to life. Now, God calls us to live in His Word system, speaking and confessing, words of blessing and life.

Chapter Nine:

A Vision With Purpose

"Where there is no vision, the people perish: but he that keeps the law, happy is he."
— **Proverbs 29:18**

In Proverbs 29:18, the profound significance of having a vision for your life is highlighted. In its original Hebrew, it suggests that without a vision, dream, or purpose, people live aimlessly. Yet, true happiness is found in those who uphold the law! When we hold God's law (or Word) close to our hearts, it ignites life and purpose within us. God's Word infuses us with meaning!

Joshua 1:8 proclaims: *"This book of the law shall not depart out of your mouth; but you shalt meditate there day and night, that you may observe to do according to all that is written there: for then you shalt make your way prosperous, and then you shall have good success."*

By immersing ourselves in God's Word day and night, we pave the way for prosperity and success! Our minds are naturally drawn to our dominant thoughts. The things we focus on most create vivid mental images, and we are ultimately attracted to these images.

This is why God encourages us in these verses to have a vision and meditate on His Word, keeping it at the forefront of our hearts and minds.

God says in Jeremiah 29:11-12: *"For I know the thoughts that I think toward you, says the Lord, thoughts of peace, and not of evil, to give you an expected end. Then shall you call upon me, and you shall go and pray to me, and I will hearken unto you."*

Imagine this: right now, God is crafting thoughts specifically for your life! He's envisioning the life you've always dreamed of, a life filled with blessings and success. God's mind is teeming with ideas of abundance and prosperity for you and your family.

In Psalm 119:130, it beautifully states, *"The entrance of Your Words gives light; It gives understanding to the simple."*

As God's Word permeates our hearts, it ignites life, faith, and revelation. It arrives during challenging times to propel you towards victory and help you overcome obstacles. Through His Spirit, God's Word and light envelop you in comfort, uplift you, and illuminate your path. Remember, Jesus declared, *"I am the way, the truth, and the life"* (John 14:6).

In Revelation 19:10, it further emphasises, *"...the testimony of Jesus is the spirit of prophecy."*

God has a message for every decision and circumstance you'll encounter. His Words are always uplifting, life-affirming, and faith-strengthening. Once more, Jesus is the way, the truth, and the life. He yearns to guide you towards the best path forward, leading you into the fulfilling plan He has for your life. By His Spirit, He will steer you towards all truth, revealing His truth in everything that matters to you—your family and your future.

Have you ever heard the saying, *"It's mind over matter"*? It's a popular phrase often used as a positive affirmation. People might dismiss it with a shrug, saying, *"Oh, that's just mind over matter! It's not real!"* But I like to twist it a bit: *"It isn't mind over matter; it's the mind of Christ over everything that truly matters to you in life!"*

God Has A Fantastic Plan For Your Life

God has a fantastic plan for your life, and He's constantly thinking about it. He's utterly in love with you. He sent His Son, the Lord Jesus Christ, to die for you and gifted you His Spirit to bring His truth, life, and revelation into your heart. God wants you to enjoy life's best moments! Jesus came to give us a fulfilling life, and He desires for us to experience it now.

I'm reminded of an Elvis Presley song, *"You Were Always on My Mind."* Today, I want to assure you that you are always on God's mind. You and your family are constantly in His thoughts, and He wants you to feel His love and salvation. He wants you to share in His divine nature and live in The Blessing of Abraham.

So, how do we embrace God's thoughts and plans for us? We must let the Holy Spirit be the guiding voice in our lives. It's the Holy Spirit who reveals our life's plan and purpose.

The Holy Spirit comes as a wonderful guide and counsellor to lead you in all truth. Trust in His leading and you will enjoy the life of Jesus Christ manifested in your own life, family, health, mind and circumstances.

We've discovered that the entrance of God's Word illuminates our path, while those without vision may perish or live recklessly. Happiness awaits those who keep the Word, and we are encouraged to meditate on it day and night.

Through this deep meditation, the Holy Spirit infuses our lives with light and vision. But what does it truly mean to meditate on God's Word?

The Hebrew word for *"meditate"* is rich with meaning, offering us a glimpse into the fullness of God's message.

When we meditate, we conjure vivid mental images and etch them onto our mind and spirit's eye. This vision allows us to see the positive outcomes we are faithfully believing for, even before they manifest. We must cultivate these mental images, thoughts, and pictures of our aspirations. By surrendering our imagination, we envision ourselves in our future with God, aligning with His plan, purpose, and destiny for us. We see ourselves as He sees us—blessed and fulfilled.

Romans 8:30 beautifully captures this journey *"Moreover whom he did predestinate, them he also called: and whom he called, them he also justified: and whom he justified, them he also glorified."*

The moment we're first saved or called by God, it's like a symphony of His voice resonating in our spirit and heart. We feel the gentle nudge of the Holy Spirit, and in response, we surrender our life to the Lord. This act of faith involves believing that Jesus Christ sacrificed Himself on the cross for our sins, rose again, and declaring Him as the Lord and Saviour of our lives. We turn away from our past mistakes and embrace His path, understanding that repentance is about changing our direction and following the way of Christ. That's why scripture proclaims Him as the way, truth, and life. By immersing ourselves in God's Word, we learn how His Kingdom truly operates. When we pray as Jesus instructed, *"Your kingdom come, your will be done on Earth as it is in Heaven"* (Matthew 6:10), we're essentially saying, *"God, we want to live life your way. Let your divine methods guide us."* We yearn to be led by His Spirit and to gain wisdom from His Son.

As James 1:22 reminds us, we aspire to be doers of the Word, not just hearers. James warns that if we listen to God's Word without taking action, we risk deceiving ourselves. God has introduced a fresh way of doing things, a new method of operation, which the Bible describes as a new way of living.

From the scripture in Romans, we understand that when we first give our life to Christ and are born-again, our name is inscribed in the Lamb's book of life. However, our minds need renewal because they've been shaped by our past experiences and thoughts. Notice how in Romans 8:30 it states that those He *"called,"* He *"justified."* We might feel unworthy, but God is making positive affirmations and declarations about you! In this passage, God sees you as *"called, saved, justified!"*

Imagine being justified in His sight, as though you had never sinned. God continues to say, *"glorified!"* After you're born-again, He perceives you differently. He never sees you the same again. He sees you as called, justified, and GLORIFIED. Reflect on that! Meditate on that! God envisions you glorified with His own Glory.

I like to say, *"When God looks at you, the Son gets in His eyes."* When God gazes upon you, His Son, who outshines any natural sun, fills His eyes. All He sees is JESUS!

Imagine a life filled with boundless love and purpose, crafted by the divine hands of God. This is the life He envisions for you, a life brimming with His incredible plans. To step into this divine plan, invite His Word into your life. Let it resonate through your ears, dive deep into your spirit, and illuminate your mind, subconscious, and heart. Allow His Word to saturate your innermost being with His thoughts and love.

God's vision is a powerful force that enters our lives through His Word and Spirit. It is born within our spirit as we meditate on His Word, conjuring vivid mental images and pictures of what He speaks concerning your today, your tomorrow, and your future. Paint these mental pictures with the colours of your health, finances, relationships, and family. Whatever holds precious value and significance to you. Use the Word of God as a seed to sow the vision, planting it firmly in your heart and mind.

Our minds are not mere word processors; they are vibrant canvases where thoughts come alive in pictures.

When I say *"fire engine,"* you don't see the letters spelled out in your mind. Instead, you envision a red truck, complete with a ladder and sirens, speeding down the highway. You see the fire engine.

Similarly, when I mention *"puppy dog"* or *"kitty cat,"* you don't visualise the words. What you do see is the fluffy, little kitty cats and the adorable puppy dogs dancing in your imagination.

This is how God desires you to capture the promises of His Word—through the power of your imagination. He wants you to create these mental pictures and then meditate on them.

But the word *"meditate"* holds more than just the creation of mental images, visions, and dreams. It also means to mutter, to speak, to think about, and to ponder. Consider this! You can mutter the promises of God. When you're alone, out walking, exercising, or working in the yard, you can repeat the promises of God and His Words about your life's circumstances over and over again. Let them become a rhythm, a melody that guides and uplifts you on your journey.

The word *"meditate"* carries the power of speech and declaration, embodying authority. God has entrusted you with dominion over your life and the environment around you. Meditating on God's Word is a crucial weapon in spiritual warfare. As scripture proclaims, *"For we wrestle not against flesh and blood, but against principalities, against powers, against the rulers of the darkness of this world, against spiritual wickedness in high places"* (Ephesians 6:12).

Our battle is not against physical adversaries but against demonic forces intent on our downfall, seeking to attack and obstruct our journey. These entities, known as the forces of darkness, wicked spirits, fallen angels, and demons, are relentless in their pursuit.

However, God has dispatched powerful angels to surround and protect you (Psalm 34:6). These angels are attuned to your declarations of faith, rooted in the Lord's Word, ready to respond (Psalm 103:20). They eagerly await your voice echoing God's truths on every matter! The only way to know God's Words is through His scripture. This knowledge unfolds as we pray over, read, and immerse ourselves in His Word, allowing the Holy Spirit to weave it into our spirit, line by line, precept by precept.

Growing up, I often heard the saying, *"Rome wasn't built in a day."* This timeless wisdom reminds us that any project worth our time, purpose, and effort requires patience and dedication. Just as athletes hone their techniques, undergo rigorous training, and follow strict diets to reach Olympic heights, we too must embrace a new way of living to achieve our dreams. If you want something extraordinary, you must step into the extraordinary and do what you've never done before!

Jesus promised us the keys to the Kingdom (Matthew 16:19), and one of those powerful keys is the influence of our words. Proverbs 18:21 declares, *"Death and life are in the power of the tongue: and they that love it shall eat the fruit thereof."* Job 6:25A echoes this sentiment, saying, *"How forcible are right words!"* And in Ecclesiastes 8:4A, we read, *"Where the word of a king is, there is power."*

A Vision With Purpose

When you were born-again, you became a king and a priest unto Jesus (Revelation 1:6). This means that where your word is, there is power! Your words have the incredible ability to bring blessings and life, to transform situations for the better. It might not happen overnight, just as Rome wasn't built in a day, but with persistence and consistency, you will cultivate the habit of speaking and mediating the right things—and it will happen! You will learn to think differently, to align your thoughts with God's Word, and to embrace a new perspective.

As we learn to think right,

we naturally learn to speak right.

We discover the importance of saying things that align with our desires and not our fears. By using words that empower the Kingdom of life, we open ourselves to blessings and abundance. Let's choose to speak things that uplift and inspire, rather than words that align with the kingdom of darkness, which seeks to take from us.

Meditation is an art of crafting mental images, envisioning your desires and how they can manifest. It's about speaking, murmuring, and muttering these visions into existence, making positive affirmations that resonate with your soul. As you feed your faith and focus your imagination on God's Word, you'll witness the impossible—mountains moving before your eyes.

Psalm 37:4 beautifully declares, *"Delight yourself also in the LORD; and he shall give you the desires of your heart."* Your mouth and tongue are powerful tools, akin to a bulldozer that reshapes landscapes. Just as a bulldozer transforms dirt into a foundation for buildings, your words can change the atmosphere around your life. By faith, you can speak and believe God's Word, altering your reality.

My wife often reminds me, *"Say it until you believe it, then say it because you believe it."* This journey is about convincing yourself, renewing your mind for God's purpose and promises. When your mind aligns with God's, you'll find yourself in harmony with His truth. Roman 3:4 boldly states, *"let God be true and every other man a liar."* Meditate on this! Decree it! Let the promises of God be your guiding light.

Fill your heart with praise and gratitude for God and His blessings. Magnify the Lord through songs and words of adoration. Sing and make melody in your heart to the Lord. Express your love and trust with your words, until they overflow from your heart. Remember, it all begins in the heart. Out of it, the issues of life proceed (Proverbs 4:23). Your mouth speaks what your heart believes (Luke 6:45).

Psalm 34:3 invites us, *"O magnify the LORD with me, and let us exalt his name together."*

And Psalm 50:23 promises, *"he that orders his conversation right, will God show to that person His great salvation."*

Isaiah 55:11 assures us, *"So shall my Word be that goes forth out of my mouth: it shall not return unto me void, but it shall accomplish that which I please, and it shall prosper in the thing where I sent it."*

What is God saying? When we praise Him and speak His Word back to Him, we return His Word to Him, full of love, trust, faith, and appreciation. This alignment with Heaven brings a manifestation of God into our lives and circumstances. Mediate on this!

Gatekeeper

Proverbs 23:7A wisely states, *"For as he thinks in his heart, so is he."* In Hebrew, *"think"* paints a picture of our natural mind as the gatekeeper to the supernatural mind—the mind of our spirit or subconscious. Your natural mind controls what enters your spirit. God wants us to let His Word, His light, His revelation flow into our spirit. It's up to us what we meditate on! What we imagine is what we create with the paintbrush of our thoughts.

Choose your vision for business, family, ministry, or life. Paint that picture and frame it with God's Word. Use His Word as the seed to infuse your dream with life and faith, causing it to germinate, grow, and mature until it becomes your reality. Through Him, you are a mountain mover, with incredible power to imagine and create.

Imagine the power of creation at your fingertips! God, the ultimate artist, breathed life into the world with just a word. And guess what? You were crafted in His image, possessing the same potential to shape your reality. So, why not speak the world you desire into existence? With the words of your mouth and the faith of your heart, let His Word inspire, guide, and empower you. Visualise it, declare it, and watch it unfold!

Revelation 12:11 reveals a profound truth: *"And they overcame him by the blood of the Lamb, and by the word of their testimony; and they loved not their lives unto the death."* This verse speaks of a victory that transcends personal experience, rooted in the divine declarations found in God's scripture. Let your testimony be a reflection of what Jesus Christ has achieved for you on the cross of Calvary, a testament to His triumph over darkness.

Colossians 2:15 celebrates this victory: *"And having spoiled principalities and powers, he made a show of them openly, triumphing over them in it."*

Jesus shattered the powers of darkness, and now He has entrusted you with His Word and Spirit. In His name, you can voice positive affirmations and declarations, transforming your testimony into His.

The Testimony Of Jesus Is The Spirit Of Prophecy!

God's appointments are confirmed through His Word, with the Spirit hovering and attesting with miraculous signs. Jesus, too, promised to be with us always, confirming His Word with signs following (Mark 16:20).

Under this covenant, when you are born-again and speak in faith the testimony of Jesus — what Christ's life and blood declare about your circumstances — you become the prophet of your own life, speaking out of faith under the Holy Spirit's anointing. You are prophesying your God-given blessings and future!

This is exactly what God desires from you! He wants His people to speak, decree, and declare His Word. Remember, it's God's will to fulfil and give you the desires of your heart as you delight in Him. So, take that step, speak the Word, and let your faith ignite the transformation you seek!

So then, when you say what God's Word says about your circumstances you are declaring Jesus' testimony about your future. His victory becomes your victory. Become the prophet of your own future by letting God and His Word be true and every man a liar (Romans 3:4).

In a nutshell, the essence of prophesy is the testimony of Jesus, and this becomes applicable in your life, when you declare the promises of God and the finished work of the cross over your life. Do this in a spirit of faith with conviction, and you are then an active prophet of your own future.

Chapter Ten:

Decree As A King

"You shall also decree a thing, and it shall be established to you: and the light shall shine upon your ways."
— Job 22:28

The demonic realm trembles when you stand firm and proclaim God's Word. Miracles aren't always instantaneous; a miracle in progress is just as powerful. But you're not destined to an endless cycle of waiting. In Jeremiah 1:12, the LORD declares, *"Then said the LORD to me, you have well seen: for I will hasten my Word to perform it."*

Picture this: Jeremiah sees the rod of an almond tree. In his part of the world, when winter arrives, all the trees shed their leaves, leaving behind nothing but dead sticks and branches, covered in ice and snow. Everything appears desolate and barren. Yet, the almond tree is the first to bud, bringing forth new life in the spring! It blossoms and blooms while other trees still look lifeless and bare.

When Jeremiah tells God he saw the rod of the almond tree, God responds, *"you have seen well"* (Jeremiah 1:12). What God is telling Jeremiah here, is: *"This a revelation, Jeremiah, an understanding. Even when everything seems dead, I am still overseeing my Word, ready to confirm it with signs that follow. Speak my Word when everything looks barren, and new life will burst forth!"*

Eyes that look are common, but eyes that see are rare. Jeremiah looked with the eyes of his spirit and saw the revelation of the power of God's Word in performance.

This is the same faith Abraham wielded. He didn't consider the deadness of his own body or the barrenness of Sarah's womb. Instead, he chose to believe God's Word. God promised him, *"I'm going to make you a father of many nations"* (Genesis 17:4).

Abraham counted God faithful, believed the promise, and trusted that God could call things into existence that didn't exist before. He believed God's Word could bring life and manifestation. Abraham became an imitator of God, and the Bible says he grew stronger in faith, not weaker (Romans 14:19-22). He glorified God and declared that God calls things that were not as though they were (Romans 4:17). God promised Abraham descendants as numerous as the stars in the night sky or the grains of sand on the ground. And Abraham believed the Word of the LORD! He decreed and declared it because God said it! I imagine Abraham saying in his heart, *"If God said it, I believe it, so that settles it!"*

Abraham was to *"see"* himself as the father of a multitude.

The Bible says that Abraham's faith was accredited to him as righteousness (Romans 4:3). When we embrace faith like Abraham's, it's also accredited to us as righteousness. Abraham called himself blessed and a father of many nations, even though in the natural, his and Sarah's bodies were far past the age of childbearing. He still believed! Why? Because God said it!

Call Things Into Being

I urge you to cling to the faith of God and Abraham. Like them, we must call things that are not in our lives, through the power and Word of God, as though they are!

God remains the God of breakthrough! (2 Samuel 5:20-21). As you cling steadfastly to your faith, unwavering in your belief, you will surely break through! Your declarations of purpose and future in God will eventually lead you to victory. For God is faithful to His promises! (Hebrews 10:23). He keeps a watchful eye and swiftly brings His Word to life, confirming and performing it with miraculous signs. It will happen for you!

Gloria Copeland in her writings, emphasises the importance of being ready to stand firm forever! Because of this mindset, your attitude, posture, and determination will show that you are prepared to stand as long as it takes. And guess what? It won't take that long. Remember, every seed produces fruit after its own kind (Genesis 1:11). It's the law of the harvest, and your faith is the seed that will grow into an abundant reality!

In Jody Hughes book, *The Kings Decree*, on page 157, Jody says *"many miracles are suddenlies because God is the God of suddenlies. He is the God of the break-through."*

Isaiah 59:19 says: *"So shall they fear the name of the LORD from the west, and his glory from the rising of the sun. When the enemy shall come in like a flood, the Spirit of the LORD shall lift up a standard against him."*

God's very breath is driving along a pent up flood of promises and revival that will sweep the Earth as a flood. It's harvest time! As the book of Amos says: *"Behold, the days come, saith the LORD, that the plowman shall overtake the reaper, and the treader of grapes him that sows seed; and the mountains shall drop sweet wine, and all the hills shall melt."*

It is time for the harvesters to overtake the sowers, and the sowers, the treaders of grape! It's time to see the seed harvested, turned into wine, and refined in a perpetual cycle of abundance with no lack. There is no force of darkness, no mountain, no law in the present, past or future, that has the power to stop or prevent the glory and the blessing God has for you through Jesus Christ!

Proverbs 23:7 intriguingly states, *"For as he thinks in his heart, so is he: Eat and drink, says he to you; but his heart is not with you."*

This verse, along with Jesus' words show us that our mouths reveal the abundance of our hearts. It suggests that while we may not always know someone's thoughts, their true nature will eventually surface through their words. The verse implies that our predominant thoughts shape who we become. As I like to say, *"As a man thinks in his heart, so he becomes!"*

To transform our future, we must be vigilant about the thoughts we entertain.

So, what are you focusing on today? Remember, Philippians 4:13 assures us, *"I can do all things through Christ who strengthens me."*

Yet, the same chapter encourages us to rejoice continually. Keep joyful thoughts at the forefront of your mind and maintain a spirit of praise and thanksgiving. Our thoughts, originating from our natural mind, influence our spiritual mind. These thoughts can either sour or fertilise our hearts. An attitude of gratitude is one of life's most powerful tools, helping us succeed through Jesus Christ.

The Bible is rich with examples of thanksgiving and praise, teaching us that praise directed to God leads to triumph. God values praise so much that He dedicated an entire book, the Psalms, to it. We are repeatedly instructed to sing praises to the Lord, as seen in Psalm 8:2, which states that God has placed His praise in the mouths of babies and young children, granting them strength.

In the spiritual realm, effective praise releases power against our enemies. Psalm 8:2 reveals that God has ordained praise for His people to counter their adversaries. By releasing praise to God, we can halt negative spiritual forces. Positive words of praise and thanksgiving, spoken through the Lord Jesus Christ, can bring these hindering forces to a standstill.

Decree As A King

Your words reveal your heart.

Jesus, in Matthew 20, affirms that out of the mouths of babes and sucklings, God has ordained strength. Psalm 22:3 reveals that God dwells in the praises of His people. Psalm 50:23 declares that offering praise to God glorifies Him and aligns our conversation with truth, life, liberty, and victory.

Through words of praise and positive affirmations from the Bible, we align our conversation with God's presence, and He reveals His great salvation to us. Philippians 3:20 reminds us that our conversation is in Heaven, from where we look to our Saviour, the Lord Jesus Christ. Verse 21 speaks of how our bodies will be transformed to resemble His glorious body, according to His working by which He is able to subdue all things to Himself.

Change Your Circumstances

Our Lord can transform any circumstance in our lives, whether from external sources or our fallen nature and carnal mind. This is why the Word emphasises the power of words and the importance of thinking and speaking rightly.

We are called to be renewed in the spirit of our mind (Ephesians 4:23), achieved through the washing of the Word and the Spirit. The Holy Spirit renews and regenerates both our spiritual and carnal minds as we fill our hearts with His Word. The significance of thinking rightly cannot be overstated.

Proverbs 23:7A declares that, *"as a man thinks in his heart, so is he!"*

The Hebrew word for *"thinks"* is *"shaar,"* and it means to calculate, reckon, estimate, or think, acting as a gatekeeper. Our natural mind is the gatekeeper to our spiritual mind. The Hebrew word *"hu"* or *"hi"* means the same, indicating that we become what we think. What we think abundantly, we will speak. Thus, if you desire something, you must speak it.

Death and life are in the power of the tongue, and this power is intertwined with our thoughts. What we focus on and dwell upon will ultimately shape us, as we release these thoughts, whether positive or negative, through the power of our spoken word.

That's why the scripture continues, *"A person can eat and drink with you, but their heart is not with you"* (Proverbs 23:7B).

I dare you today to take a moment and reflect: where is your heart with God? Is the Word of God the cornerstone of your life? Have you truly valued His Words more than your daily sustenance? Recall Jesus' powerful declaration, *"Man shall not live by bread alone but by each word that comes from the mouth of God."* (Matthew 4:4)

Consider Philippians 3:20, where it states that our conversation is in Heaven. Your words are a window to your soul, revealing your true identity and the path you're on. The disciples couldn't help but share the incredible things they had witnessed and experienced—the miracles and wonders of Jesus Christ's life! This miraculous journey is laid bare in the Word of God for all to behold. We can witness the transformative power of the Word and how the Spirit of faith can move mountains through spoken words. If you believe in your heart and express it with your mouth, remember to say it until you believe it, then say it because you believe it!

Cultivate positive images of yourself, your family, and your future. Build these vibrant pictures in your natural mind, and as you do, the Holy Spirit will infuse them into your heart or your supernatural mind, the mind of your spirit. Romans 8:30 tells us, *"Moreover whom he did predestinate, them he also called: and whom he called, them he also justified: and whom he justified, them he also glorified."*

See yourself as God sees you—not just called, not just justified, but glorified. Embrace your identity as a victor in life through the Word and Spirit of the Lord Jesus Christ. The word *"conversation"* in Philippians 3:20, in Greek, is *"po-lee-yoo-mah,"* meaning to live as a citizen of Heaven. It connects to the Kingdom of God, urging you to live as a citizen of His divine realm. The Kingdom is a realm of power, dominion, and authority. The Bible proclaims that the Kingdom of God reigns supreme over all. God desires you to speak and live as a king unto Him.

Remember, Jesus is the King of Kings and the Lord of lords. According to His Word, because you are born again and washed in His blood, you are called to be a king and priest unto God through Jesus Christ. You are destined to reign and rule in life through Him.

Satan is a conquered enemy, vanquished by the powerful Word of the Lord Jesus Christ. This Word continues to triumph over Satan today! The Bible describes the Word of God as a *"sharp two-edged sword"* (Hebrews 4:12).

In Psalm 149:5-9, it exhorts: *"Let the saints be joyful in glory; let them sing aloud upon their beds. Let the high praises of God be in their mouth, and a two-edged sword in their hand. To execute vengeance upon the heathen, and punishments upon the people;*

To execute upon them the judgment written: this honour have all his saints. Praise you the LORD."

Psalm 150:6 echoes this call, saying, *"Let every thing that has breath praise the LORD. Praise you the LORD."*

The apostle Paul encourages us to always be rejoicing, full of joy, and praising God (Philippians 4:4), because the Lord is always near to assist. Paul advises us to focus on things that are lovely, honest, true, just, pure, and of good report (Philippians 4:8). Reflect on your past victories in God, express gratitude for the small blessings and miracles in your life, and be thankful for the breath in your lungs that allows you to praise God. He says, if there be any praises, think on these things! As you meditate on this great promise of God, the God of peace shall be with you.

In Joshua 1:8, it states, *"This Book of the Law shall not depart from your mouth; but you shall meditate in it day and night, that you may be careful to do according to all that is written in it. For then you will make your way prosperous, and you will have good success."*

"Beloved, I wish above all things that you may prosper and be in health, even as your soul prospers." — *3 John 1:2*

Our soul is a vibrant tapestry woven from our mind, will, and emotions. The thoughts we nurture, the ideas we dwell on, and the meditations we embrace deeply influence our soul, mind, will, and emotions. God's Word is a powerful force that fortifies our will, renews our mind, and ignites positive emotions in our lives. It is the ultimate source of life, love, joy, happiness, comfort, and ultimate victory. In John 10:10, God promises us life in all its abundance, contrasting it with Satan's intentions to steal, kill, and destroy. However, Jesus offers life of superior quality and overflowing quantity. Psalm 89:15 proclaims, *"Blessed is the people that know the joyful sound: they shall walk, O LORD, in the light of thy countenance."*

Praise, rooted in God's Word and directed to Him through the Lord Jesus Christ, is a joyful sound that halts the work of the evil one and his cohorts in the spiritual realm. According to Philippians 4, our giving becomes part of our Heavenly conversation. It is deeply connected to our heart and its attitude. When God is our source and we trust Him to meet our needs, we give joyfully and abundantly without fear. God loves a cheerful giver who is prompt and whose heart is fully engaged in their giving (2 Corinthians 9:6-7). Whether we give ourselves in service, submission, praise, adoration, and through our finances to support the ministry and spread the gospel, it becomes part of our Heavenly conversation. The apostle Paul assures us that this produces fruit that abounds to our account.

"Not because I desire a gift: but I desire fruit that may abound to your account" (Philippians 4:17).

Your Account In Heaven

Imagine having an account in Heaven, a place where every word you speak and every action you take, every dollar you give, is recorded. Jesus Himself highlighted this, saying we will give an account of every word we speak (Matthew 12:36). Our words are like threads in a tapestry, revealing our true selves to the Father. Your acts of giving are woven into this divine conversation. The Greek word for *"account,"* is, *"logos."* It is the same word used for *"words,"* highlighting the profound connection between our speech and our life.

The Bible teaches us that our heart is where our treasures lie (Matthew 6:21). We invest our finances in what we desire, believe, and are committed to—what brings us joy and fulfilment. When we cheerfully praise God and worship Him through tithes and offerings, we are enriching our heavenly account, just as we would our earthly bank account. God promises not just blessings, but a 30, 60, 100-fold return and life everlasting!

Every word, action, thought, and belief is visible to God, becoming part of our Heavenly conversation. In the Roman world of Paul's time, citizenship was a badge of honour, and the word *"conversation"* signified kingdom citizenship. You are a citizen in the Kingdom of God (Philippians 3:20). For early Christians, this was a powerful metaphor, resonating with their identity. As Romans paid tribute and pledged allegiance to their empire, so we identify and give our allegiance to God's Kingdom. We are citizens of the Great King, subjects of the Almighty, His children, and kings and priests of Jesus Christ through His blood.

Through giving, living, thinking, confessing, and meditating, through praise, we affirm our Kingdom citizenship—our Heavenly citizenship. We declare our allegiance to it. And in Philippians 4:19, Paul assures us that God shall supply all our needs according to His riches in glory!

Imagine living by every single word, no matter how small it might appear. Each word holds the potential to nourish our souls and bring life to our spirits. So, don't let them slip away unnoticed. Take time to meditate on each word, extracting every truth from every verse as you delve into them one by one. Declare your victory from the divine Word, as God unveils it to you through His Spirit. Speak the words God has for you regarding every situation you encounter, or are about to face. Stand firm, unwavering, without worry or doubt. Instead, let your voice rise in praise! Words of praise, brimming with faith and gratitude, are the celestial language of Heaven. Recall the teachings of Jesus in the Lord's Prayer, where He instructed us to pray, *"Let your Kingdom come, let your will be done on Earth as it is in Heaven"* (Matthew 6:10). Our mission, our calling, is to saturate the Earth with words from God's Word —life-giving words that carry the essence of Heaven.

The Secret Power Of The Tongue

Chapter Eleven:

Intimacy

"But the people that do know their God shall be strong, and do exploits."
— **Daniel 11:32B**

Discovering the essence of a vibrant, Word-filled life begins with a deep connection to God. This journey unfolds through His Word, rich with promises that guide and inspire us. By engaging in prayer, meditation, and study, we draw closer to Him, nurturing an intimate bond.

In the natural world, intimacy springs from a genuine curiosity about another person—their passions, their quirks, their joys, and their sorrows. We become close to someone by investing time in their company, sharing meaningful conversations, and experiencing life together. Through these interactions, we uncover the secrets of their heart and what truly brings them joy. Effective communication and quality time are crucial in building such a relationship. When you first encounter the love of your life, you begin to share common interests and appreciate the unique aspects of their being. You build intimacy by understanding and speaking their love language, and by actively supporting it. This connection is strengthened by actions and words that reflect your heart's desires and priorities. How you hold the other person in your life and the size of the piece they occupy in your heart all influence the depth of your intimacy.

Just as the Bible encourages us to study and show ourselves approved to God (2 Timothy 2:15), we discover His love through His Word and the promises He has made. The profound sacrifice of His Son on the cross of Calvary reveals how much God cares for us. Remember, Jesus Christ died for us—the godly for the ungodly, the righteous for sinners—to boldly demonstrate and declare God's love.

I often say, "Faith is the currency of Heaven. Praise is the language of Heaven. Love is the atmosphere of Heaven. And joy is the strength of Heaven."

Intimacy

In Romans 14:17, it beautifully states, *"For the kingdom of God is not meat and drink; but righteousness, and peace, and joy in the Holy Ghost."*

The Holy Spirit, the Spirit of freedom and love, is the third person of the trinity and the Spirit of God. Love is a vibrant expression of Heaven, and the fruits of the Spirit flow from it. Love is encapsulated in the fruits of the Spirit. Righteousness is the path of believing, doing, and living correctly. It is a precious gift from God, achieved through Jesus Christ's work on the cross. Righteousness is the Kingdom of God manifesting within you.

James 3:18 wisely notes, *"And the fruit of righteousness is sown in peace of them that make peace."*

When you are born-again, you become the righteousness of God in Christ, a child of God seated in a Heavenly place with Jesus. God has called and empowered you to live and reign in life through the Lord Jesus Christ. In His name, and through faith in His name, every blessing of God becomes yours— It's yes and amen! It's yes and amen in Him!

You are the seed of Abraham through Jesus Christ (Galatians 3:29), and Abraham's blessing is now yours. You have inherited The Blessing of Abraham. As Proverbs 10:22 assures, *"The blessing of the LORD, it makes rich, and he adds no sorrow with it."* You don't have to pay for it; Jesus Christ did that with His life and blood at Calvary. You just have to believe, because Jesus bought it all for you!

Today, I encourage you to believe for the unbelievable and expect to receive the impossible, all because of what Jesus did. God desires for you to know Him.

The apostle Paul passionately declared, *"That I may know him, and the power of his resurrection, and the fellowship of his sufferings, being made conformable unto his death"* (Philippians 3:10).

Jesus Our Executor

Picture this: we embrace the blessing, decree, and declare victory over our lives, a victory Christ secured for us through His sacrifice. He rose from the dead, took His place at God's right hand, and now executes His own will. He has entrusted us with the power of attorney, the authority to speak in His name, to watch as mountains of adversity crumble and victory unfolds.

I love to play with the concept of intimacy, breaking it down like this: what God is saying is, *"Into-me, you will see."* To fellowship with God is to engage with His Word through His Spirit. Pray into the Word, speak it, and meditate on it day and night, for God and His Word are one. As you delve deeper into the Word, the Spirit ignites understanding and revelation in your heart, drawing you closer to God. The more you know God, the more intimate you become with Him, and as this intimacy grows. He opens your eyes to understand and births revelation of His Word into your spirit and heart through His Spirit. From this intimacy, you become an empowered spirit-speaking being. You were created to be a spirit-speaking being, born-again to win. Born again to echo what God says and, through faith and patience, see it established and manifested in your life.

Daniel 11:32B says, *"but the people that do know their God shall be strong, and do exploits."*

Even though, you may think you know God or understand His ways, through study and meditation Of His Word you can become firmly established in the truth and know the reality of God in your life. We must learn to apply God's Word to life's situations by becoming a doer of the Word. In Daniel 11:32, the word *"know"* is the Hebrew word *"yada,"* it means, *"to know, to perceive, to understand, to acknowledge,"* meaning *"to come to know or recognise!"*

The more you become intimate with God, the more you will come to know Him and be able to fully recognise Him and His ways. Through this intimacy and knowledge, you will become more empowered to do the greater exploits that Jesus spoke of, through His name.

Acquaint Yourself With Him

We must get acquainted with Him to accomplish and reveal His glory in the Earth. To further expand and develop, the Hebrew word *"yada,"* describes intellectual awareness and experiential knowledge and intimate familiarity. In Biblical context, *"yada"* often implies a deep, personal and relational knowledge, such as the intimate relationship between God and His people. Or between individuals.

In ancient Hebrew culture, knowledge was not merely intellectual but was deeply relational and experiential. It involved knowing someone in a holistic, spiritual way or dimension. *"Yada"* also described the intimate relationship between between a husband and his wife, as well as the convent relationship between God and His people.

I encourage you to become intimate with God, get to know Him more.

I think of the scripture in Philippians 3:10 *"That I might know Him and the power of His resurrection and the fellowship of His sufferings, becoming conformable unto His death."*

The Secret Power Of The Tongue

Chapter Twelve:

Angels Operate This Way

"The Lord has prepared his throne in the heavens; and his kingdom rules over all. Bless the Lord, you his angels, that excel in strength, that do his commandments, hearkening unto the voice of his Word. Bless you the Lord, all you his hosts; you ministers of his, that do his pleasure. Bless the Lord, all his works in all places of his dominion: bless the Lord, O my soul."
— Psalm 103:19-22

Before crafting humanity, God brought angels into existence. Just as He entrusted Adam with the task of naming every creature, assigning destiny through the power of words, God had already bestowed names upon His angels. These celestial beings held various ranks and authorities, each with distinct roles within God's Kingdom and realms of dominion. They were assigned specific missions to fulfil on God's behalf.

The verse above highlights their remarkable strength, a gift from God along with all the resources they needed to accomplish their divine duties. Angels were commanded to obey God's commandments and to attentively listen to the voice of His Word. As stunning creations, they served as God's ministers, servants, and heavenly ambassadors, tasked with carrying out His will. One of God's greatest desires was to shower His children with the promises of His Kingdom.

Luke 12:32 reassures us, *"Fear not, little flock; for it is your Father's good pleasure to give you the kingdom."*

The Bible introduces us to a fascinating array of angelic beings, with three particularly captivating figures. First, there's Lucifer, once a celestial luminary who succumbed to darkness and defied God's will. Then we encounter Michael, the formidable Archangel, who valiantly battles on God's behalf.

Revelation 12:7 vividly describes this celestial conflict: *"And there was war in heaven: Michael and his angels fought against the dragon; and the dragon fought and his angels."*

This passage reveals a stark contrast between the righteous angels led by Michael and the malevolent ones under the command of Satan, the fallen Lucifer, also known as the dragon.

The third intriguing angel is Gabriel, the harbinger of revelation, who delivered profound prophecies and future events to the prophet Daniel, as well as Mary, heralding the birth of Jesus.

The Bible also paints a vivid picture of seraphim and cherubim, along with winged beasts and wondrous creatures. It speaks of watchers who descended from Heaven and guardian angels dispatched to serve and protect God's people. Hebrews 1:14 eloquently states, *"Are they not all ministering spirits, sent forth to minister for them who shall be heirs of salvation?"*

In Ephesians, we delve into the realm of principalities, powers, and the rulers of darkness in this world, as well as the spiritual wickedness in high places:

"Finally, my brothers and sisters, be strong in the Lord, and in the power of his might. Put on the whole armour of God, so that you may be able to stand against the tricks of the devil. For we do not wrestle against flesh and blood, but against principalities, against powers, against the rulers of the darkness of this world, against spiritual wickedness in high places. Therefore take unto you the whole armour of God, so that you may be able to withstand in the evil day, and having done all, to stand. Stand therefore, having your loins girt about

with truth, and having on the breastplate of righteousness; And your feet shod with the preparation of the gospel of peace; Above all, taking the shield of faith, with which you shall be able to quench all the fiery darts of the wicked. And take the helmet of salvation, and the sword of the Spirit, which is the Word of God: Praying always with all prayer and supplication in the Spirit, and watching thereunto with all perseverance and supplication for all saints" (Ephesians 6:10-18).

Picture this: a realm where angels, divine creations of God, once thrived in perfect harmony with His Purpose, Word, and Will. These celestial beings were attuned to the voice of the Word of God, diligently carrying out His commandments. However, the narrative took a dramatic turn when Lucifer, in a bold act of rebellion, led a third of these angels into a coup against God. His ambition was nothing short of overthrowing God's throne and seizing control of the entire kingdom, including all worlds and dominions created by God.

These angels functioned on a word system, a system that still governs them today. God's Word reigns supreme. Just as Adam and Eve were entrusted with dominion over the world and tasked with subduing any enemies of God, you too are called to exercise dominion over these fallen and rebellious beings. The forces of darkness, as described in

Ephesians 6, including Satan and his cohorts, are not to be feared. The Bible assures us that we are more than conquerors through Him who loves us (Romans 8:37).

Jesus Christ, who loves you deeply, went to the cross for you and defeated these enemies on your behalf. He has granted you authority over every power of the evil one and his forces of darkness through His written Word. By believing in Him with your heart and speaking with your mouth, "*Jesus is Lord!*" you can wield this authority.

In the name of Jesus, you as a king through His authority, now have the power to subdue, control, and bring into subjection all the enemies power. Jesus has given you dominion over all of Satan's power. Just as God speaks His Word and the angels heed it, when you speak the Word in Jesus' name, the angels will carry out your command, bringing you into victory. Even after Satan's fall, two-thirds of the angels continue to serve God's purpose! These angelic forces are sent by God to protect, watch over, and minister to His servants—those born-again through the name of Jesus. Even new believers possess the power to bind and loose, as Jesus declared in Matthew 18:18, "*Truly I say unto you, Whatever you shall bind on earth shall be bound in heaven: and whatever you shall loose on earth shall be loosed in heaven.*"

Through the power of attorney, you have the authority to use the name of Jesus. Jesus Christ is the commander and chief of Heaven's armies. He has granted you the right, in His name and through His Word, to command the angels. When you speak God's Word, these angels of light gain strength, and Satan's power is defeated. As 1 John 5:4 states, *"For whatever is born of God overcomes the world: and this is the victory that overcomes the world, even our faith."*

When you pray in Jesus' name, you are issuing commands to angels. Speaking in His name also gives commands to angels. As you pray in the Holy Spirit and speak the Word of God in other tongues, the angels hear and understand God's will and plan for your life. They know God's purpose for you and work through the power of God's Word to bring you safety, victory, and success.

Let's Explore The Word Of God

Hebrews 1:14 says, *"Are they not all ministering spirits, sent forth to minister for them who shall be heirs of salvation?"*

Psalm 34:7 states, *"The angel of the LORD encamps round about them that fear him, and delivers them."*

Psalm 91:11-12 assures us, *"For he shall give his angels charge over you, to keep you in all your ways. They shall bear you up in their hands, lest you dash your foot against a stone."*

Psalm 91:1-4 declares, *"He that dwells in the secret place of the most High shall abide under the shadow of the Almighty. I will say of the Lord, He is my refuge and my fortress: my God; in him will I trust. Surely he shall deliver you from the snare of the fowler, and from the noisome pestilence. He shall cover you with his feathers, and under his wings shalt you trust: his truth shall be your shield and buckler."*

In verse 2, God instructs us to declare by faith that He is our refuge and fortress, in whom we trust. As we make these declarations, believing in our hearts and confessing His Lordship with our mouths, the Word promises that He delivers us from every attack and pestilence. He provides a protective covering with His wings, and His Word becomes a shield and buckler. A buckler is a small round shield used for protection in ancient times; it symbolises God's protection and faithfulness, offering a shield to those who trust in Him.

Psalm 91:5-6 continues, *"you shalt not be afraid for the terror by night; nor for the arrow that flies by day; Nor for the pestilence that walks in darkness; nor for the destruction that wastes at noonday."*

We need not fear any situation that operates in darkness or seeks to attack us. I encourage you to read and memorise Psalm 91 and declare it over yourself and your family.

Chapter Thirteen:

Confessing God's Word

"Let us hold fast the confession of our faith without wavering; (for he is faithful that promised;)"
— **Hebrews 10:23**

There are two interesting words in the Hebrew language that illustrate very powerfully the mind of God and His power released in the beginning to create and bring creation as we know it into manifestation. These two powerful words are: *"A-Bara"* (meaning, *"I will create"*) and *"ke-Dab'ra"* (meaning, *"as I speak"*). This is how God brought the whole of creation into manifestation. He created as He spoke and the Holy Spirit moved on the words that He spoke to bring what he said into manifestation.

Today, when children play magic games or pretend to be magicians, they use the phrase *"abracadabra."* It's like when a magician pulls a rabbit out of a hat. Essentially, it appears he's pulling something out of nothing. These words used by magicians originally came from these two Hebrew words and the concept of God creating the seen out of the unseen. Through faith, we now understand that the worlds were created by faith. Through the Word of God. The visible from the unseen, invisible substance of faith. And that's why this teaching on confession is so powerful.

Confession is a powerful act of alignment with God's Word. It's about echoing the truths that He has spoken and embracing them as our own. When we confess, we are essentially agreeing with God, acknowledging His wisdom and authority in our lives. It is saying the same thing God says!

Imagine holding onto a precious promise. To truly grasp it and make it a reality, we must repeat it, meditate on it, and let it permeate our hearts. This is what it means to hold fast to our confession. We say what God has said, over and over, until we are fully persuaded that what God has promised He is able to perform. We say it until we believe it, then we say it because we believe it! Without confession, there can be no possession of God's promises.

As believers, we are blessed with incredible rights in Christ. These are not mere privileges but profound truths that shape our identity and destiny. We are called to affirm these rights constantly, to testify to them, and to witness to the tremendous biblical facts that support them. The apostle Paul, in his letter to Philemon, encourages us to let our faith become effective by acknowledging every good thing that is in us through Christ Jesus (Philemon 1:6).

Affirmations of Truth

Our lips should be a constant source of affirmations of truth. We are to hold fast to these truths without wavering, letting them be the foundation of our faith and the guiding light of our lives. However, wavering in our confession can have serious consequences. It means denying ourselves the promise and the performance of it, missing out on the blessings that God has in store for us.

Let us stand firm in our confession, unshakeable in our faith, and always prepared to declare the truths that God has revealed. By embracing this steadfastness, we invite a life brimming with His promises and the joy of seeing them fulfilled.

As the scripture in James 1:6-7 reminds us, *"But let him ask in faith, nothing wavering. For he that wavers is like a wave of the sea driven with the wind and tossed. For let not that man think that he shall receive any thing of the Lord."* This passage underscores the importance of a resolute faith, free from doubt, as the foundation for receiving God's blessings.

The Psalmist echoes this sentiment, urging, *"Let the redeemed of The Lord say so"* (Psalm 107:2). This call to affirm our redemption is a powerful reminder of the grace and mercy that have transformed our lives. Moreover, in Psalm 40:16, we are encouraged to *"Let all those that seek you rejoice and be glad in you: let such as love your salvation say continually, The LORD be magnified."* This is a daily invitation to celebrate our salvation and to magnify the Lord through our words and actions.

So, what truths should we affirm constantly? We should speak the positive scriptures that reveal the good things within us, in Christ. There are countless affirmations we can make daily as we engage with the Word.

Consider these:

- God is who He says He is.
- I am who God says I am.
- God can do what He says He can do.
- I can do what God says I can do.
- God has what He says He has.
- I have what God says I have.

Christianity is often referred to as the Great Confession, as all aspects of our faith in Christ—salvation, healing, deliverance—are rooted in our verbal affirmation of Jesus' Lordship. This Lordship extends over everything we encounter today, offering us strength and guidance.

Fight The Good Fight Of Faith!

Paul, in his letter to Timothy, encourages us to *"Fight the good fight of faith, lay hold on eternal life, whereunto you are also called, and have confessed a good confession before many witnesses"* (1 Timothy 6:12).

This passage is a call to action, to remain committed to our faith, and to continue proclaiming the good news of Jesus Christ to the world. The scripture instructs us to fight the good fight. A good fight is one you win! You strive fervently in your confession until the thing believed and confessed is fully possessed.

Let us embrace this journey with faith and joy, continually affirming the truths that God has spoken and magnifying His name in all we do.

Matthew 12:34 says, *"O generation of vipers, how can ye, being evil, speak good things? for out of the abundance of the heart the mouth speaks."*

It is our sacred duty to fill our hearts with the divine Word of God, the teachings of Christ. The scriptures offer us guidance on how to achieve this profound connection. Colossians 3:16 beautifully instructs us, *"Let the Word of Christ dwell in you richly in all wisdom; teaching and admonishing one another in psalms and hymns and spiritual songs, singing with grace in your hearts to the Lord."*

The responsibility lies with us to embrace this journey. In this above scripture, to *"dwell"* means, to *"linger deeply in thought and speech, to make it our home, to reside there."*

Wisdom is essential to succeed in all areas of life. It is basically the ability to use knowledge effectively for your benefit through life.

"Richly" signifies, *"abundance, an overflowing presence."* Psalms is joyful singing of God's praises, and hymns are forms of verbal confession!

The heart, not the mind, is the key. Remember, we are a triune being: spirit, soul, and body. We need to believe with our heart and speak with our mouth.

The Word then renews our mind. You can live righteously in your heart and still have wrong thoughts in your head. What truly matters is what resides in your heart. We strive to believe with our hearts because we are born-again.

2 Corinthians 10:4-5 says, *"For the weapons of our warfare are not carnal, but mighty through God to the pulling down of strong holds; Casting down imaginations, and every high thing that exalts itself against the knowledge of God, and bringing into captivity every thought to the obedience of Christ."*

We replace the negative, fearful or fruitless thoughts and imaginations with the Word of God. The mind thinks in pictures, so we need to create positive pictures through productive thoughts using what God says in His scripture. As we do this, our imagination will go from negative leaning and thinking to positive believing, and seeing the desired result! It's a positive, mental image that we create in our imagination or thought-life and then confess it out with the words of our mouth.

Let us actively open our hearts to receive the Word of God. Jesus, who is the Word, stands at the door of our hearts, gently knocking. It is up to us to open the door and welcome Him in. As we do, He enters in the form of His Word and power, guided by His Spirit. Through meditation, the Holy Spirit will unlock the faith and revelation within that word, allowing it to grow and flourish in us. Jesus Himself declared in Romans 10:8-10:

"But what says it? The Word is near you, even in your mouth, and in your heart: that is, the Word of faith, which we preach; That if you shall confess with your mouth the Lord Jesus, and shalt believe in your heart that God has raised him from the dead, you shalt be saved. For with the heart man believes unto righteousness; and with the mouth confession is made unto salvation."

Romans 10:17 says, *"So then faith comes by hearing, and hearing by the Word of God."*

You need to learn to listen to your heart (spiritual understanding) and not your mind (the natural understanding). Believing in your heart and speaking with your mouth, gets the job done. Not believing with your mind. Don't worry about your mind, it will be renewed by the Word (and eventually come into alignment with our heart and mouth).

Your heart, your spirit, is a new creation. It can believe, and wants to believe, God's Word!

Our recreated spirit is designed by God to believe. However, our minds must be renewed. This takes place by the Word of God as we put it into practise and study it. By becoming a doer of the Word not a hearer only.

Once again, Romans 10:9-10 says, *"That if you shall confess with your mouth the Lord Jesus, and shall believe in your heart that God has raised him from the dead, you shall be saved. 10 For with the heart man believes unto righteousness; and with the mouth confession is made unto salvation."*

2 Corinthians 5:17 says, *"Therefore if any man be in Christ, he is a new creature: old things are passed away; behold, all things are become new."*

Renew Your Mind

Romans 12:2 says, *"And be not conformed to this world: but be you transformed by the renewing of your mind, that you may prove what is that good, and acceptable, and perfect, will of God."*

Titus 3:5 says, *"Not by works of righteousness which we have done, but according to his mercy he saved us, by the washing of regeneration, and renewing of the Holy Ghost."*

Ephesians 5:26 says, *"That he might sanctify and cleanse it with the washing of water by the Word."*

Romans 3:3-4 says, *"For what if some did not believe? shall their unbelief make the faith of God without effect? 4 God forbid: yes, let God be true, but every man a liar; as it is written, That you might be justified in your sayings, and might overcome when you are judged."*

The word *"judged"* in the above scripture, is the word *"tried."* It paints a picture of you in a court of law being tried by a prosecuting attorney. The devil, or Satan, is the accuser of the family of God. He comes to steal, to kill, and to destroy. He comes to plant doubts, wicked imaginations, fears, and worries into your mind. Because those seeds, if they are allowed to grow, will produce weeds and other problems in your life and affairs.

We need to replace, these negative seeds with positive seeds of life and victory. Joshua 1:8 says, *"This book of the law shall not depart out of your mouth; but you shall meditate there day and night, that you may observe to do according to all that is written there: for then you shall make your way prosperous, and then you shall have good success."*

The word *"meditate"* here in this verse is the Hebrew word, *"hagah."* It means, *"to meditate, to murmur, to ponder, to speak, and to utter."* So we can see, from this meaning of this Hebrew word, it involves both the heart or spirit (imagination) and the mouth and the tongue in speaking and uttering. It has also other meanings, that convey the idea of, *"to care for, reflective consideration."* It's a sound and/or a frequency. It's the act of meditating God's laws, His works (seeing what He does, or, watching what He does). And, His Words. Suggesting a deep internalised engagement with divine truths. This is how we attend to God's Word.

Remember, your thoughts are like clouds, a frequency that you project out, that go and gather up results for you good and bad. You are then drawn to your predominant thoughts or thinking processes. So, think God's Words, picture His promises. Send out good vibes, thoughts and words, to gather up good or God results.

The Secret Power Of The Tongue

Chapter Fourteen:

Frequency

"My soul longs, yes, even faints for the courts of the LORD: my heart and my flesh cries out for the living God."
— **Psalm 84:2**

As you delve into Psalm 84, you'll first encounter a captivating instruction for the chief musician. This Psalm is a special offering from the sons of Korah, and the term *"chief musician"* evokes the image of a choir director, lead supervisor, or overseer. Throughout the Psalms, you'll find intriguing inscriptions beneath each Psalm number, revealing who the Psalm is addressed to, its intended audience, or even the day it should be performed. For example, Psalm 90 is a heartfelt prayer penned by Moses, the revered man of God. These descriptions are a hallmark of the Psalms, and Psalm 84 is no exception, as it is directed to the chief musician or overseer.

In the grand symphony of life, you are the chief musician and overseer of your life.

The Bible is rich with references to songs, musicians, and musical instruments. Imagine the triumphant return of Jesus, who will gather us home with a mighty shout, accompanied by the voice of the archangel and the trumpet of God (1 Thessalonians 4:16). The power of song and victory cries, whether through instruments or voices, holds immense significance for both God and your personal journey. Musical instruments and songs of praise and thanksgiving were integral to the construction of the temple and the vibrant ministry that followed. In the Old Testament, when the Israelites prepared to face their adversaries, the singers and musicians would lead the charge. The Bible speaks of a deliverance sound, known as songs of deliverance. In Psalm 100:1-5, it joyfully proclaims:

"Make a joyful noise unto the Lord, all the lands. Serve the Lord with gladness: come before his presence with singing. Know you that the Lord he is God: it is he that has made us, and not we ourselves; we are his people, and the sheep of his pasture. Enter

into his gates with thanksgiving, and into his courts with praise: be thankful unto him, and bless his name. For the Lord is good; his mercy is everlasting; and his truth endures to all generations."

We're called to make a joyful noise to the Lord, a symphony of praise and thanksgiving that echoes across the globe. Psalm 100:2 invites us to *"Serve the Lord with gladness and come before His presence with singing."* As we enter His gates, we do so with gratitude, and as we step into His courts, we bring praise and a heart full of thanks, blessing His name. Psalm 105:1-2 further encourages us to: *"O give thanks unto the Lord; call upon his name: make known his deeds among the people. Sing unto him, sing psalms unto him: talk you of all his wondrous works."*

The Psalmist passionately urges us to sing to Him and to share the stories of His incredible deeds.

You Are The Conductor Of Your Own Life's Melody

Every music group, choir, or worship team has a chief musician, guiding the harmony and rhythm. Even the angels have one. Before his fall, Satan, known then as Lucifer, was the chief musician, worshipping in God's presence and filling it with songs and psalms of praise.

Lucifer held this role until his rebellion led to his downfall. When Lucifer, the once-chief musician and anointed cherub, was cast out, God created humanity: Adam and Eve. He blessed them with His spoken Word, granting them the power to rule over all creation by speaking the same words God speaks. Adam named the animals, and their names have endured through the ages. For millennia, sheep have been sheep, cattle have been cattle, and so on, because Adam had the authority to steward the Earth and reign through God's Blessing. Adam was destined to be the chief musician of his life and the garden.

In essence, humanity stepped into Lucifer's shoes when he fell. Cast out from God's presence, he lost the ability to fill it with worship. Through his disobedience and rebellion, he became a fallen, corrupted being. Once known as the anointed cherub, Satan is now replaced by God's people, who are anointed. It's the Church that carries the anointing today! Under the old covenant, God anointed prophets, kings, judges, priests, individuals, and leaders with His Spirit. Now, under the new covenant, we are all anointed by the Holy Spirit to bring praise, worship, and thanksgiving to God. We are to be the kings and priests who honour, thank, and worship

God through music and other beautiful words of praise using the voice He has entrusted to us.

God has entrusted you with a powerful voice to guide and shape your life. Embrace this gift by crafting an environment in your home and beyond, rich with words of faith, love, encouragement, and gratitude.

These words should uplift and inspire, infusing life and healing wherever they go. We are called to invite God's presence into our lives through worship and praise, for as Psalm 22:3 beautifully states, God dwells in the praise of His people. His Spirit is alive in the songs, prayers, and thanksgiving that we offer. Even if singing isn't your forte, every person possesses a voice capable of making a joyful noise unto the Lord. This sound is a celebration of all that God has accomplished, is currently doing, and will continue to do for us.

Each individual has the power to speak words of life and blessing. It's up to us to choose our words, beliefs, and attitudes. Just as Lucifer had free will, so do we. While he chose rebellion and failure, we have the chance to succeed, remain faithful to the Word, humble ourselves under God's mighty hand, and triumph in life through Jesus Christ.

Ephesians 5:18-19 encourages us to be filled with the Spirit of God and to speak to ourselves in psalms, hymns, and spiritual songs. It guides us to create a melody in our hearts for the Lord and to always give thanks for everything in the name of Jesus Christ, while submitting to one another in the fear of God.

Now, let's delve into the profound message of Ephesians 6:10-19:

"Finally, my brethren, be strong in the Lord, and in the power of his might. Put on the whole armour of God, that you may be able to stand against the wiles of the devil. For we wrestle not against flesh and blood, but against principalities, against powers, against the rulers of the darkness of this world, against spiritual wickedness in high places. Therefore take unto you the whole armour of God, that you may be able to withstand in the evil day, and having done all, to stand. Stand therefore, having your loins girt about with truth, and having on the breastplate of righteousness; And your feet shod with the preparation of the gospel of peace; Above all, taking the shield of faith, wherewith you shall be able to quench all the fiery darts of the wicked. And take the helmet of salvation, and the sword of the Spirit, which is the Word of God: Praying always with all prayer and supplication in the Spirit, and watching thereunto with all perseverance and supplication for all saints;

And for me, that utterance may be given unto me, that I may open my mouth boldly, to make known the mystery of the gospel."

Arm Yourself!

In the Word of God, we are called to put on God's armour, equipping ourselves to resist the devil's cunning military tactics. Ephesians 6:12 reveals that our struggle is not against physical beings but against spiritual forces—principalities, rulers of darkness, in wicked places. The Greek word for *"wrestle"* implies *"vibration,"* which can also mean perception. So, we don't perceive or vibrate against flesh and blood but against these spiritual entities.

When we sing, vibrations occur as air flows over our vocal cords. These vibrations prompt us to shape our mouths into syllables and sounds, which we can either speak or sing. We can channel these sounds towards principalities, powers, and forces of darkness. By speaking words of life in the name of Jesus, we are actively dismantling, binding, and neutralising the works of the kingdom of darkness.

Moreover, we can wear the helmet of salvation, which includes all of God's promises. This signifies that we are now God's children, born again. It's essential to have these thoughts shielding and protecting our mind, as our thoughts are crucial to our life. Our thoughts and mindset are significant because the natural mind is the guardian of the supernatural or subconscious minds of the spirit. This will be explored in another chapter.

In 2 Corinthians 10:5, it states, *"Casting down imaginations, and every high thing that exalts itself against the knowledge of God, and bringing into captivity every thought to the obedience of Christ."*

By wearing the helmet of salvation and safeguarding our thought life, we dismantle every imagination and thought that rises against the knowledge of God. This pertains to the Word as it relates to you, your situations, and circumstances. We can eliminate negative words of darkness and fortify our minds with the Word of truth and God's promises. We can replace negative thoughts and the enemy's thoughts with God's thoughts and Words. Our thoughts for God's thoughts.

Isaiah tells us that God's thoughts are higher than ours, and His ways are higher than our ways (Isaiah 55:8-9). When we swap our thoughts for God's thoughts, we start being led by the Holy Spirit into the right path, God's path, the path out of problems and into blessings. The Bible declares that those led by the Spirit of God are the sons of God

(Romans 8:14). God is showing us that He desires to lead and guide us every day through life.

There's a path that seems right to us, but it leads to destruction. In contrast, the ways of God are filled with peace, healing, and deliverance (Proverbs 14:12). While our hearts hold their own plans, Yahweh or the Lord is the answer to our words. It's our duty and responsibility to prepare our hearts before Him. God has equipped us with the ability to plan and provided us with eyes, ears, and minds to use for His glory.

Commit Your Ways To God

God weighs people's spirits. By committing our ways and works to Him, He will straighten our paths. As we nourish ourselves with His Word, it becomes the regulator, the standard, and the guiding line for life. The Bible reminds us in Psalm 119:9, *"How can a person make their way clean? By giving heed to the Word of God."*

God empowers us to achieve great things in life. We do this by taking action, becoming as James 1:22 says, doers of the Word, not hearers only. It warns that if we hear God's Word and don't act, we deceive ourselves. But if we heed and perform His Word, we are blessed in the doing. Our works become established, and we accomplish much for God, fulfilling our purpose in life. God has a purpose for every person's life. You are His dream, His idea, and He has a plan for you, and it's all good. When we mess up, we have Jesus the righteous to advocate for us. God sent His Son to deliver us, to die in our place, and set us free from sin so we can be born-again to newness of life in Jesus. He sends His Holy Spirit to work out His plan of salvation in our lives as we yield and give ourselves to Him.

God knows the plan He has for us to prosper, to give us hope and a future, not to harm us in any way (Jeremiah 29:11). God is a good God and desires to do us good. The Bible declares in John 10:10 that it is the devil who comes to steal, kill, and destroy; but Jesus came to give life and life abundantly! He does this through His Spirit and His Word.

In Ephesians chapter 6 verse 12, we are reminded that we wrestle against spiritual forces of evil in the heavenly realms. Satan comes to knock us out of our place, but the Holy Spirit restores our equilibrium through the Lord Jesus Christ, bringing us back to the life, liberty, and freedom we were meant to have.

Psalm 67:5-7 calls for people to praise God, saying, *"Then shall the earth yield her increase; and*

God, even our own God, shall bless us. God shall bless us; and all the ends of the earth shall fear him."

God Wants To Bless You

God wants to bless us and for all the Earth to fear and respect Him. It's the enemy, Satan, and fallen spirits that come to curse and destroy. God also tells us in Psalm 67:2 that He desires to see His saving health and prosperity spread to all the nations of the Earth. Jesus died for all people, all families, and in every nation, those who fear God and outwork righteousness, will be accepted by Him. A vibration is a powerful force; one of the most powerful known to man. When tectonic plates shift and rub, it causes vibrations to spread through the earth, land, and sea. This can lead to destructive effects, like tsunamis, tidal waves, and buildings toppling. We can witness the power and life-changing impact of an earthquake, both on land and under the sea, as it releases very destructive forces.

When we learn to sing and speak in faith, we unleash powerful forces against the kingdom of darkness. Our high praises of God can stop, slow down, and obliterate the works of evil. Have you ever felt the energy of a place? An informal term for vibration is a person's emotional state, the atmosphere of a location, or the connection of objects, as felt by others. People say, *"I felt the vibes. Could you feel it too?"*

You are the conductor of your life, tasked with creating positive energy and atmosphere in your home and wherever you go. You are called to transform the atmosphere by bringing God's presence into the scene. As I write this, I think of the Beach Boys' song about good vibrations. I'm sure many of you have heard it. It's time for the Church to release the good vibrations of the Kingdom and the Heavenly atmosphere into the Earth!

Nicola Tesla once wrote, *"If you want to find the secrets of the universe, think in terms of energy, frequency, and vibration."* Einstein said, *"Everything in life is a vibration."* Every atom or molecule in the universe vibrates at a specific frequency.

Every living person is constantly vibrating! At a molecular level, at a particular frequency. That frequency is its home. Today, we often ask, *"Does that resonate with you? Did that speak to you? Can you relate to that?"* It's time for the Church, the people of God, to resonate with the Kingdom of Heaven and the vibrations and sounds emanating from God's throne. There is a sound from the throne today. It is the sound of joy, the sound of victory, and the song of salvation!

Vibrations & Frequency

Vibration is a back-and-forth motion. Frequency is the number of vibrations in any given unit of time. We measure frequency in hertz. Sound is also measured in hertz. Sound is the molecular essence of vibration. The Bible says, *"Deep calls unto deep"* (Psalm 42:7). The deep things of God, by the Spirit of God, are reaching out to the deep things in your heart. You, in your reborn spirit, are calling to the deep things of God.

The Bible states that the Holy Spirit makes intercession for us by groaning (Romans 8:26). These are the deep callings of God in our spirit, where the Holy Spirit cries and intercedes on our behalf to the Father through the Word. In these deep groanings of vibration and frequency sounds that are flowing from your spirit, by the Holy Spirit, the plans, will, and purposes of God are being birthed and made known to you, by the Holy Spirit. The Holy Spirit takes the counsel of God, His mysteries and divine secrets and reveals them to your spirit and mind. You become one with God through the Lord Jesus Christ and the power of the Holy Spirit.

As you yield to God by yielding to his Word, and praying in the Holy Spirit, through the gift of tongues (more on this in my book, Life's Changing Principles for Victorious Living). He — the Holy

Spirit — is the illuminator. He illuminates God's plans and purposes to your heart. Filling your heart with the desires of God's heart for your life, as you fill your heart with the Word and sounds of Heaven. Revealing to you how to win in life through Jesus Christ.

In physics, sound is vibration that travels as an acoustic wave. Through a medium like gas, liquid, or a solid. Water for example, you can see vibrations form on water and the rings spread out. As born-again Christians, we can influence the very water in our bodies by studying, meditating, singing the Word, and singing in the Spirit. We can sing in the Spirit and not only impact our being but also the atmosphere around us.

Have you ever entered a house where tension had just been released? After you leave, you say, *"Did you feel the atmosphere?"* It was palpable. The words spoken and sounds released before your arrival shaped the atmosphere you encountered. You can also leave a conversation or group and ask your friend, *"Was what they spoke about resonating with you?"* Did you sense the energy or frequency of that meeting?

God is a faith God, and God is a word God. God created this universe, this world, through the spoken Word. When God created trees and plants, He spoke to the Earth. When God created fish and sea creatures, He spoke to the sea. But when God created us, He spoke to Himself. We emerged from God, we were crafted from God, and when He formed us from the dust of the ground, He breathed Himself into us, and people became a living, talking spirit. God is a living, talking spirit, and we are created in His image as living, talking spirits. The Bible tells us in Psalm 89:15, *"Blessed is the people that know the joyful sound: they shall walk, O LORD, in the light of thy countenance."*

Salvation isn't just a concept; it's a tangible reality and a powerful sound. It's the melody of blessedness, the symphony of happiness, joy, and bliss. God's joyful sound is a mighty blast, a shout, and even a call to battle. It's a trumpet's call, a joyful sound designed to dismantle the forces of darkness, vanquish Satan and his schemes against you, your family, your business, and your life, while bringing God's promises to life. That's why we must declare God's decrees, confess His Word, and align with Heaven's decrees, for the power of life and death lies in our words. I urge you to make joyful sounds, sounds of praise and thanksgiving to God, sounds of deliverance and prosperity. The Bible assures us that when we magnify the Lord, we align our lives with His. We magnify Him, and He reveals His salvation to us.

Water And Consciousness

Consider this: the Word of God instructs us to renew our minds by washing them with His Word. Have you ever thought about how water can hold thoughts and emotions? It's intriguing! Our bodies are approximately 60% water, and there's more to it than meets the eye. Dr. Masaru Emoto's research indicates that the molecular structure of water is influenced by the words and emotions directed at it. Given that we are mostly water, how vital are the words we use towards ourselves and our family, remembering that you are the overseer, chief musician, and choir director of your life? Emoto found that water exposed to positive words and intentions formed beautiful, symmetrical structures when frozen. In contrast, water exposed to negativity developed disorganised, asymmetrical structures.

Dr. Emoto also explored the impact of sound on water. His research showed that certain sounds, like classical music, create intricate patterns. In contrast, heavy metal music led to unpleasant distortions. Isn't it fascinating how these studies emphasise the importance of the words we hear and the music and atmosphere we cultivate in our lives? These elements are essential for our overall well-being, affecting us psychologically, mentally, and spiritually. Since we are greatly composed of water, the sounds we listen to influence us. It's no wonder Jesus advised, *"Be careful what you hear"* (Mark 4:24).

What you hear can penetrate your spirit and impact your life. The Bible tells us in Psalm 84:4-5, *"Blessed are they that dwell in thy house: they will be still praising thee. Selah. Blessed is the man whose strength is in thee; in whose heart are the ways of them."*

God desires us to live in His presence, rejoicing forevermore and praising continually. The Lord assures us He is our sun and shield. He will grant us grace and glory, and He will withhold no good thing from those who walk upright. Verse 12 is our response: *"O LORD of hosts, blessed is the man that trusts in you."*

I encourage you today to underline things in this book, look up scriptures, and place your trust in God's Word. He loves you, and His plan is all good.

The Secret Power Of The Tongue

Chapter Fifteen:

A Bold Challenge — Don Gossett[1]

Let me challenge you today, to make a quality decision, never again to have a wrong confession but instead to agree with, to affirm, and confess what God's Word says about anything which may arise in your life in the days to come.

- Never again confess defeat, for "...*God... always causes us to triumph in Christ....*" (2 Corinthians 2:14).

- Never again confess bondage, for "...*Where the Spirit of the Lord, there is liberty*" (2 Corinthians 3:17).

- Never again confess sickness, for "...*With his stripes we are healed*" (Isaiah 53:5) and "... *He took our infirmities, and bare our sicknesses*" (Matthew 8:17).

- Never again confess fear, for *"God has not given us the spirit of fear; but of power, and of love, and of a sound mind"* (2 Timothy 1:7).

---
[1] Used with permission.

- Never again confess, *"I can't,"* for *"I can do all things through Christ which strengthens me"* (Philippians 4:13).

- Never again confess doubt and lack of faith, for *"...God has dealt to every man the measure of faith"* (Romans 12:3).

- Never again confess weakness, for *"..The Lord is the strength of my life..."* (Psalm 27:1) and *"...The people that do know their God shall be strong and do exploits"* (Daniel 11:32).

- Never again confess Satan's supremacy over your life, for *"...Greater is he that is in you, than he that is in the world"* (1 John 4:4).

- Never again confess a lack of wisdom, for *"But of him are you in Christ Jesus, who of God is made unto us wisdom..."* (1 Corinthians 1:30).

- Never again confess feelings of guilt, for *"There is therefore now no condemnation to them which are in Christ Jesus..."* (Romans 8:1) and *"As far as the east is from the west, so far has he removed our transgressions from us"* (Psalm 103:12).

- Never again confess worry, for *"Casting all your care upon him; for he cares for you"* (1 Peter 5:7).
- Never again confess discontent, for *"...For I have learned, in whatsoever state I am, there to be content"* (Philippians 4:11).

- Never again confess loneliness, for Jesus said *"...I will never leave you, nor forsake you"* (Hebrews 13:5) and *"... Lo, I am with you always, even unto the end of the world"* (Matthew 28:20).

- Never again confess a fear of the future, for *"No Eye has not seen, nor ear heard, neither have entered into the heart of man, the things which God has prepared for them that love him. But God has revealed them unto us by his Spirit..."* (1 Corinthians 2:9, 10).

- Never again confess an inability to conquer sin in your life, for *"the law of the Spirit of life in Christ Jesus has made me free from the law of sin and death"* (Romans 8:2).

- Never again confess frustration, for *"You will keep him in perfect peace, whose mind is stayed on you..."* (Isaiah 26:3).

- Never again confess confusion, for *"Now we have received, not the spirit of the world, but the spirit which is of God; that we might know the things that are freely given to us of God"* (1 Corinthians 2:12) and *"For God is not the author of confusion, but of peace..."* (I Corinthians 14:33).

- Never again confess failure, for *"No, in all these things we are more than conquerors through him that loved us"* (Romans 8:37).

Chapter Sixteen:

Great Achievements

"I can do all things through Christ which strengthens me."
— **Philippians 4:13**

The greatest achievements, all began just as dreams. These achievements were in the hearts of people who dreamed. Then they took action, by believing and speaking their dreams into reality. The oak tree rests inside the acorn, the bird awaits in the egg. Dreams are the seedlings of realities. My wife, Kerrie, often says, *"Your dreams don't have a use-by date."*

Leonardo Da Vinci, was an illegitimate child, which in his day and culture was a big deal! Which severely limited his opportunities in life, at that time. Yet at the age of twelve, he vowed, *"I shall become one of the greatest artists the world has ever known, and one day I shall live with kings and work with princes."*

Napoleon Bonaparte, as a young child, spent long hours mentally conquering Europe, dreaming of how he would lead and manage his troops. The rest is history.

The Wright Brothers transformed their dreams into airplanes. Henry Ford turned his vision, of an affordable car for everyone, into a manufacturing assembly line. As a child, Neil Armstrong aspired to make his mark in aviation. Then, in July 1969, he became the first man to walk on the moon.

The Importance Of Dreams

Everything begins with a dream, so if you've never had one, you've never experienced a dream come true. Remember, no matter your age, it's never too late to become what you could have been; it's never too late to see your dreams fulfilled. It's time to rise up with faith in your heart and start expressing your desires and the visions God has woven into them, and watch those dreams and desires take shape with the Word of God, thereby shaping your future with the spoken promises of God.

I like to say, "If you want something you've never had, you have to do something you've never done."

Great Achievements

In the Bible in the Book of Job 22:28 we read, *"You shall also decree a thing and it shall be established unto you..."*

Don Gossett's best selling book, out of the 120 books that he wrote, was the book titled, *"What you say is what you get."*

1 Thessalonians 5:3 says, *"And the very God of peace sanctify you wholly; and I pray God your whole spirit and soul and body be preserved blameless unto the coming of our Lord Jesus Christ."*

The meaning of the word sanctified here in the Greek, is *"qa-dosh"* and it is pronounced *"kah-dosh."* This word means, holy, sacred, set apart. I want to hone in and do a deep dive on what it means to be sanctified.

Through the born-again experience, your spirit has been made holy, and you have been set apart by God for a special purpose. This term *"set apart"* signifies a separation from the common to the uncommon. God has an uncommon call on your life! You are unique, one of a kind, and the only one of you that God has. You have been endowed with the seeds of greatness, designed for accomplishment, and engineered for success by God. Born-again by the Spirit of God, He wants to use you for His purpose. He has a plan for your life, aiming for you to achieve things that no one else on Earth can do as well as you can, because you are a unique individual.

Every person born-again is born to win, to succeed, and to overcome. The Bible tells us that this is the victory that overcomes the world, even our faith (1 John 5:4). And our faith is not just our own; it is God's faith being birthed in our hearts by the Holy Spirit when we gave our lives to Christ.

God has great things for you to achieve for His Kingdom, wherever He has called or placed you in life. You are called to function from that place, and God has a wonderful love plan for your life. His plan is one of goodness, blessing, and wholeness for you and your family. Your best is still to come! As Ecclesiastes says, *"Better is the end of a thing than the beginning thereof."* You are heading for your best days of your best life!

Now that you are born-again, your spirit is renewed and transformed in Christ (2 Corinthians 5:17). Your spirit is holy, and God's Holy Spirit resides within you. By accepting Him, you have also embraced His will and His grand love plan for your life. To truly experience and live this great life that God has designed for you, you need to gain revelation and understanding of His plan. This revelation and understanding comes from the Word, the Bible, as you study it, and it is revealed to you by the Holy

Spirit. It is your responsibility to dedicate your soul—mind, will, and emotions—to the purposes of God and His Kingdom.

Everything Begins With The Blessing

God has given us everything through The Blessing of Abraham, and it is ours to enjoy abundantly. However, by faith, it is our responsibility to claim these blessings. We do this through belief in our hearts and the words we speak with our mouths.

As we begin this journey, we must let the Holy Spirit of Christ reign in our hearts and minds. By allowing the Holy Spirit to guide you and rule in your heart, and by bringing your mind into alignment with God's Word and Will, as it states in 2 Corinthians 10:4-5, *"For the weapons of our warfare are not carnal, but mighty through God to the pulling down of strong holds; casting down imaginations, and every high thing that exalts itself against the knowledge of God, and bringing into captivity every thought to the obedience of Christ;"*

As you set your spirit and mind to the purposes and will of God, your body will naturally follow. By aligning your spirit, mind, and body with the Holy Spirit, you can overcome the desires of the flesh through renewing your mind in God's will and Word.

This process transforms you from a mere hearer of the Word into a doer. As James 1:25 in the Bible states, you will be blessed in your actions! By aligning yourself with the Kingdom, you follow the example of Peter in the Gospel of Matthew. Peter allowed the Father in Heaven to reveal to him who Jesus truly was.

Matthew 16:15-19 says:

"He said unto them, But whom say you that I am? And Simon Peter answered and said, you are the Christ, the Son of the living God. And Jesus answered and said unto him, Blessed are you, Simon Barjona: for flesh and blood has not revealed it unto you, but my Father which is in heaven. And I say also unto you, you are Peter, and upon this rock I will build my church; and the gates of hell shall not prevail against it. And I will give unto you the keys of the kingdom of heaven: and whatsoever you shall bind on earth shall be bound in heaven: and whatsoever you shall loose on earth shall be loosed in heaven."

As you align yourself with the Kingdom, God's Word and will, you begin to receive God's best. Remember, Jesus said, *"But seek first the kingdom of God, and his righteousness; and all these things shall be added unto you"* (Matthew 6:33).

Great Achievements

God has blessed us with an amazing ability to imagine. In the book of Ezekiel, it refers to the image chambers of our hearts (Ezekiel 8:12). This power exists in both our supernatural and natural minds, allowing us to imagine and create. We can use this power to form words, and by faith, with the right believing and speaking patiently, we can bring these words into reality, or, as a Hebrews 10:36 says, receive the promise. It's important to remember that our mind doesn't always think in words; it thinks in pictures. All these pictures, imaginations, and visions start with thoughts—words that become thoughts, which then become pictures. We learn to speak words of life from God's Word. As the scripture says in Philippians 2:5A, *"Let this mind be in you, which was also in Christ Jesus."*

Success On Every Level

Great achievers understand four key things about the imaginatory mind that God has created for us. To succeed on every level, you need to know these four aspects of your mind and imagination:

1. Your mind constantly acts on what it believes you want. If it perceives that acting in your best interest will lead to your desired life, then you must change your behaviours to align with this. If your current situation is not what you want, it indicates a

lack of proper collaboration with your mind. To collaborate effectively and achieve your best life, you need to renew your mind through behavioural changes, focusing on thinking, meditating, and speaking the right things.

2. Your mind is naturally inclined to seek pleasure and avoid pain. This is why you strive to avoid pain to survive. Personal trainers often say, *"No pain, no gain,"* emphasising the need for discipline in pursuing your goals. A disciplined follower is someone who delays gratification. Consider an Olympic swimmer who delays many pleasures to rise early, train for hours, and fine-tune their diet and habits like sleep etc, to concentrate on their dreams. Paul describes this as keeping our bodies under control so we can receive the prize of God's blessing and glory.

3. To receive God's best and life's best, it comes down to two things: the images you create in your mind and the way you feel about yourself. The words you think and say about yourself, your life talk, will penetrate your spirit—your inner self. You will become a product of your predominant thoughts and feelings about yourself. The Bible states, *"As a man thinks in his heart, so is he,"* or, as I personally like to say, *"so he or she becomes"* (Proverbs 23:7).

4. Your mind loves what is familiar and is programmed to repeat it. To succeed at any level, you must make the familiar, unfamiliar, and the unfamiliar; familiar.

If you put these 4 things into practice in your life, you will have good success across the board, you can have success at any and every level. Proverbs 21:23 says, *"Whoever keeps their mouth and their tongue, keeps their soul from troubles."*

Matthew 12:34-37 says:

"O generation of vipers, how can you, being evil, speak good things? For out of the abundance of the heart the mouth speaks. A good man out of the good treasure of the heart brings forth good things: and an evil man out of the evil treasure brings forth evil things. But I say unto you, That every idle word that men shall speak, they shall give account thereof in the day of judgment. For by you words you shall be justified, and by your words you shall be condemned."

From these sentences, once again, we see how powerful the words of our mouth are and how they affect our life.

Malachi 2:17 says:

"You have wearied the LORD with your words. Yet you say, Where have we wearied him? When you say, Every one that does evil is good in the sight of the LORD, and he delights in them; or, Where is the God of judgment?"

Our thoughts, opinions, conversations, and the beliefs in our hearts can actually weary the Lord, as suggested in the above verse. Take a moment to consider that. Have you ever been around someone whose conversation tired you out? We need to ensure that our conversations don't weary the Lord. I'm not referring to sharing your heart's problems with God. I'm talking about an attitude, as seen in Malachi, where we hold wrong judgments, ideas, and thoughts about people and God, and we express those things. These attitudes of heart and mind, conveyed through thoughts or words, can truly tire the Lord. In Malachi 3:13, the Lord says, *"Your words have been stout against me, yet you say, 'What have we spoken so much against you?'"*

The word *"stout"* here means to bind, conquer, and restrain God. Reflect on this for a moment: your words have the power to conquer and restrain God. They don't prevent God from running the universe or the greater world we live in, but they can hinder, restrain, or conquer God from working in your personal world, your sphere of influence. You might wonder, *"Why aren't I seeing the victory of the LORD in my life?"* You could think, *"If I have The Blessing of Abraham and Jesus has done all this for me at the cross, then why aren't I experiencing this new victorious life?"* You might ask, *"Why isn't this working or happening for me?"* To which I would respond: the first thing you need to do is examine your heart attitude, your imagination, your beliefs in your heart, and what you're saying with your mouth about today and your tomorrow. What are you thinking and feeling about yourself in your inner-man? In your thought life?

In Malachi 3:14-18 it says:

"You have said, It is vain to serve God: and what profit is it that we have kept his ordinance, and that we have walked mournfully before the Lord of hosts? And now we call the proud happy; yes, they that work wickedness are set up; yes, they that tempt God are even delivered. Then they that feared the Lord spake often one to another: and the Lord hearkened, and heard it, and a book of remembrance was written before him for them that feared the Lord, and that thought upon his name. And they shall be mine, says the Lord of hosts, in that day when I make up my jewels; and I will spare them, as a man spares

his own son that serves him. Then shall you return, and discern between the righteous and the wicked, between him that serves God and him that serves him not."

I challenge you to conduct a personal check-up. Examine your heart, mind, motives, and words, using the Word of God. If you have believed, spoken, or thought the wrong things, ask God for forgiveness and apply the blood of Jesus to them. Thank God that they are washed away and cleansed by His blood. Remove the weeds of incorrect thoughts, motives, and words from your heart and cast them into the sea of God's forgetfulness. As Philippians 4:8 states, *"Finally, brethren, whatsoever things are true, whatsoever things are honest, whatsoever things are just, whatsoever things are pure, whatsoever things are lovely, whatsoever things are of good report; if there be any virtue, and if there be any praise, think on these things."*

Respect

Fear God and respect Him. Honour His Word and share His goodness with your family and friends. As scripture says, when you fear and honour Him, when you think on His name, and when you speak in line with His Word, God is writing a book of remembrance (Malachi 3:16). Your conversations are being recorded in His books in Heaven (Philippians 3:20).

Remember, your words have the power to either weary or empower a situation. Every great achiever recognises this. Once you understand the power in your words, you'll be mindful of what you say. Similarly, understanding the power of thoughts and imagination will make you cautious about what you think. Recognising the power of presence will guide you to be careful about where you are. Lastly, understanding the power of focus will help you be deliberate with what you do.

In James 3:2-6 it says:

"For in many things we offend all. If any man offend not in word, the same is a perfect man, and able also to bridle the whole body. Behold, we put bits in the horses' mouths, that they may obey us; and we turn about their whole body. Behold also the ships, which though they be so great, and are driven of fierce winds, yet are they turned about with a very small helm, wherever the governor lists. Even so the tongue is a little member, and boasts great things. Behold, how great a matter a little fire kindles! And the tongue is a fire, a world of iniquity: so is the tongue among our members, that it defiles the whole body, and sets on fire the course of nature; and it is set on fire of hell."

And, *"But the tongue can no man tame; it is an unruly evil, full of deadly poison"* (James 3:8).

And, *"Who is a wise man and endued with knowledge among you? Let him show out of a good conversation his works with meekness of wisdom"* (James 3:13).[2]

Take Control Of Your Tongue

No one can control your tongue, not even God. You must control it yourself. Your tongue can be set on fire by thoughts of life from Heaven or thoughts of death from hell. Remember, John 10:10, the enemy comes to steal, kill, and destroy, but Jesus comes to give you life, and that life more abundantly. God wants you to enjoy this abundant life. However, to enjoy this life, it is your decision—our decision—what fuel we add to our hearts to energise our tongues.

I pray that as you study and read this book and the scriptures within, you will allow the fire of God from Heaven, by the power of the Holy Spirit, by using the Word of God, to set your heart and tongue on fire for Jesus and His Kingdom.

---

[2] I recommend reading the whole of James chapter 3 as it has powerful revelations concerning our tongue.

Great Achievements

You can enter into God's best and be someone who makes a difference in life by being an ambassador of Christ and spreading the good news of the Kingdom. I also encourage you to read Psalm 64, as it once again gives us insights into how the power of the tongue works for people.

Words have power, every football coach at half-time knows the power of words and uses them for their best advantage. Games can be won or lost, by the words that the coach uses to inspire his team at half-time.

However, God's Words have more power than just inspirational power. They have creative power, they are full of faith, they are faith-containers! In fact, the universe was created out of the faith-verse!

Words have the ability to create positive things or negative things. As it says in Proverbs 18:21, death and life are in the power of the tongue! In Amos 3:3, we read, *"Can two walk together except they be agreed?"*

Agree With God

We must agree with God, by agreeing with the Word. Say what God says, by saying what the Word says. Now let's look at what God's number one desire is for your life, that's found in 3 John 2: *"Beloved, I wish (desire) above all things that you may prosper and be in health, even as your soul prospers."*

To give you a little more understanding of the above verse, we will look at couple of words from the original Greek. Firstly, the word *"beloved"* is *"ag-ap-ay-tos,"* which means, *"beloved, dearly loved, well loved,"* meaning you are *"dear to Him"* or the *"best."* God is calling you His best!

The Greek word *"wish"* in the above scripture, means *"to pray, to will, to wish."* Implying it is God's deepest desire, His Will for you to prosper.

The word *"above"* means, *"above, beyond, excess, over, completeness."*

The word *"all things"* means, *"all, any, every, the whole whatever or whosoever."*

The word *"prosper"* means, *"to help you on the road to success in searching."* It means to, *"succeed in business affairs, and to have a prosperous journey."*

The word *"health"* means, *"sound health, to well and to be saved."*

Soul here, is *"your soul and your spirit."*

God is desiring you to prosper and to be in health in the physical realm, in the same way your soul and spirit will prosper through a relationship with God; through prayer and an understanding of His Word.

God is interested not just in your spirit and soul in the eternal life to come, but He is fully interested and fully invested in your prosperity, both spiritually, mentally, socially, and physically today, now, and through all the days of your life.

The Secret Power Of The Tongue

Chapter Seventeen:

Don't Quit!

"In all these things we are more than conquerors through him that loved us"
— **Romans 8:36**

Your own resolve to not quit is more important than any other one thing. Many years ago, I came across a quote that said, *"If you're going through hell, don't quit, keep going."* If you've spoken the wrong words, made incorrect confessions, or have a habit of speaking negatively about your circumstances, family, and situations, don't panic and think it's too late. Instead, ask God for forgiveness, repent for those wrong and negative words, and commit to speaking right and positive words.

Just as you would spray weed-killer in a garden to eliminate weeds and allow good grass to grow, you can apply the blood of Jesus over those wrong words, asking God to forgive you and render them ineffective. Then, make a conscious decision to speak the right words!

To find the right words that we need to speak, that will bring life and blessing to our circumstances or the circumstances of those around us, all we have to do is turn to Gods Word. The Bible, the Holy Scriptures, are full of exceeding and precious promises that God has provided for us to empower us to win in life through Jesus Christ.

Think of your phone. These days, phones are filled with apps and other programs to help you solve life's problems. Every single time they release a new phone, they are always improving on and updating its capabilities. Everything from a compass to maps, GPS, calculator, phone, diary, camera, banking, health, fitness, media and entertainment and the list goes on. However, in order to benefit from the applications that are found in your phone, or can be downloaded to it, you must take the phone out of your pocket, turn it on, and activate it! Then, apply the app to the required task.

Well, in the same way, your Bible is full of the life-giving promises of God. Jesus said, *"Man shall not live by bread alone, but by every word that proceeds from the mouth of God"* (Matthew 4:4). God's Word is powerful and life-giving! It is filled with incredibly great and precious promises that God has made to you.

When you apply these promises to your life and circumstances, they can transform your situation, moving you from disadvantage to favour. Just as a phone needs to be taken out of your pocket, turned on, and the app applied, you need to take the Bible out of your pocket, find the specific promise that relates to your need or situation, and apply it!

Focus on what God has said about your situation. Meditate on it and apply it by speaking that specific promise out loud. Address the problem directly! Command that mountain to move and be cast into the sea! (Mark 11:23).

Remember, the blessings and promises from God's Word are voice activated. The power lies in the spoken word, especially when spoken with faith. Understanding that, *"The Blessing is voice activated!"* is a key to victory in life.

Abraham's Seed

I have been confessing the scripture that says: *"If you be Christ then are you Abraham seed and an heir of the promise"* (Galatians 3:29). The Bible tells us in Romans 10:17 that faith comes by hearing, and hearing by the Word of God. As we repeatedly confess God's Word, we are building an image of that word or promise into our spirit.

The Bible promises that as you hear God's Word, faith will come to you. So, by confessing the promise over and over, you are releasing the revelation and faith of that promise into your spirit. The Bible says, the heart believes, and then your mouth confesses what your heart believes (Romans 10:10). For out of the abundance of your heart, your mouth will speak (Luke 6:45).

What you have abundantly put into your heart is what will come out of your mouth in life's process. When the pressure is on, if you have filled your heart with negativity, worry, and fear, those negative thoughts will come out. But if you have filled your heart with the positive, life-giving assurances of God's Word, then those positive words and thoughts will emerge. Jesus said, *"Therefore I say unto you, Whatever things you desire, when you pray, believe that you receive them, and you shall have them"* (Mark 11:24).

If we believe in our heart and confess with our mouth what the Word says, then we can have the very thing that we confess or say. This is how you got born-again! You believed in your heart that Jesus is God and that He died on the cross for your sins, and as you confess that belief that Jesus is now your Lord and Saviour, the Word says, you are saved! So then, with the heart, man believes, and with the mouth, confession is made unto salvation. The very thing that you say in faith, believing in your heart, will manifest and come to pass. And that is why, God said that death and life are in the power of your tongue! (Proverbs 18:21).

God intended for every day to be a blessing for us, His creation. This blessing has been active on Earth since its inception. However, it is crucial that we comprehend it and learn how to apply it, as it is not automatic in our lives. Each day, through our thoughts and words, we choose between The Blessing and the curse. This choice is evident in our lives and society today.

Each of us who have accepted Jesus as the Lord of our life, have been blessed. This Blessing accompanies us every morning, empowering us to overcome seemingly impossible situations that may arise daily. With The Blessing's power, you can persevere through challenges that might lead others to quit. However, this Blessing is activated by faith and voice. You must fill your heart with faith by first hearing God's promises and then speaking them out until all doubts and fears fade away. Trust in God and His Word, His promise to you. God loves you and wants you to succeed in life! He created you in His image, and from Genesis, we see that the first thing God did for people was to bless them and give them dominion over all adverse circumstances in this world (Genesis 1:26-28). God blessed and empowered people by speaking over them, ensuring their future was one of victory and enjoyment. Due to sin, people lost their authority and dominion. Through sin, we became subject to the curse and were removed from the Garden of Eden and its Blessings. Yet, our Lord loved us so much that He sent His only Son, Jesus Christ, to die in our place and restore us to a life of dominion, victory, and joy.

Jesus has granted us the authority and power of attorney to speak in His name, proclaiming God's promises to overcome any curse or adverse circumstances that may come your way. The Holy Spirit desires to reveal to your heart the power of the spoken Word, both positive and negative, and how it can influence the course of your entire life. Additionally, the Holy Spirit wants to show you the power contained in God's promises, which are delivered to you through the Lord Jesus Christ and His Word. Through this revelation and its application, you and your family can live the life you dreamed of and enjoy The Blessings provided by God.

Remember Galatians 3:29: *"If you belong to Christ, then you are Abraham's seed and an heir to the promise."* I encourage you to pray and ask the Holy Spirit to reveal the power of the spoken Word through your tongue. John 16:13 states, *"When the Spirit of truth comes, he will guide you into all truth. He will not speak on his own; he will only speak what he hears, and he will tell you what is yet to come. He will glorify me because he will receive from me and show it to you."*

Here, we see that one of the Holy Spirit's desires is to guide you into all of God's truth. He will help you understand the heavenly conversations between the Father and the Son. Jesus is the Word made flesh, and the Holy Spirit will glorify the Lord Jesus Christ. He will take all the promises God made to Jesus and bring the power and revelation of those promises into your life, mind, heart, and understanding. The Holy Spirit does this so that you can apply God's Word and promises and win in life through Jesus Christ. In John 16:23-24, we read a powerful promise from Jesus: *"That day you will not ask me anything. Truly, truly, I tell you, whatever you ask the Father in my name, he will give you. Until now, you have not asked anything in my name. Ask, and you will receive, that your joy may be complete."*

Whatever we ask the Father in the name of Jesus Christ, He will give it to us. Before we knew Jesus as our Lord and Saviour, we didn't ask for anything in His name. Now, we have the revelation that we are joint heirs with Jesus Christ and heirs of The Blessings God promised Abraham (Romans 8:17). We can claim these Blessings as our own by asking the Father for them through Jesus' name and speaking them over our lives and circumstances with faith in our hearts, because that Blessing is voice activated!

The blessing is voice activated!

Chapter Eighteen:

Abraham's Seed

"And if you are Christ's, then you are Abraham's descendants, and heirs according to the promise."
— **Galatians 3:29**

"For you know the grace of our Lord Jesus Christ, that, though he was rich, yet for your sakes he became poor, that you through his poverty might be rich."
— **2 Corinthians 8:9**

God promised to bless Abraham, multiply him, and increase him greatly. In my book on The Blessing of Abraham, I explore seven powerful promises that God made to him. These promises are now available to us through Jesus' sacrifice on the cross of Calvary. Jesus died for us so that we could inherit Abraham's Blessing.

Galatians 3:13-14 states, *"Christ has redeemed us from the curse of the law, being made a curse for us: for it is written, Cursed is everyone that hangs on a tree: That the blessing of Abraham might come on the Gentiles through Jesus Christ; that we might receive the promise of the Spirit through faith."*

Don't Worry

Stay firm! Worrying is a form of wavering. The Bible advises us in Hebrews 10:23, *"Let us hold fast the confession of our faith without wavering; (for he is faithful that promised;)."* To hold fast to the confession of our faith without wavering, you must learn to maintain your faith regardless of external circumstances or feelings. In James 1:6-8 the Word says, *"But let him ask in faith, nothing wavering. For he that wavers is like a wave of the sea driven with the wind and tossed. For let not that man think that he shall receive any thing of the Lord. A double minded man is unstable in all his ways."*

One way we waver is by speaking words that contradict God's Word or our beliefs. If we realise we've done this, we need to repent of those negative words, ask God for forgiveness, and nullify them by thanking Him for the blood of Jesus, which forgives all sin. Romans 14:23B states, *"For whatsoever is not of faith is sin."*

God desires us to live by faith, trusting in Him, His love for us, and His Word. He has made precious promises to us through the life and blood of Jesus. Hebrews 12:24 highlights, *"To Jesus the mediator of the new covenant, and to the blood of sprinkling, that speaks better things than that of Abel."* This shows that the blood of Jesus and its achievements on the cross of Calvary speak great things about your life! Among these, it declares that you are forgiven, the barrier separating you from God has been removed (Ephesians 2:14), you are a new creation in Christ (2 Corinthians 5:17), God's child (1 John 3:2), Abraham's seed, and an heir of the promise (Galatian's 3:29). Additionally, God's Word promises a bright future for you (Jeremiah 29:11). You don't have to remain where you are today. You can move upward and onward because you are Blessed!

Say What God Says

You just need to declare what God says and what the blood says! In Revelation 12:11, it states, *"And they overcame him by the blood of the Lamb, and by the word of their testimony; and they loved not their lives unto the death."* We conquer the evil one through the blood of Jesus Christ, the Lamb of God, and the word of our testimony!

What is your testimony today? Are you speaking about what the circumstances say about your life? Are you talking about what your bank account says about your life? Are you mentioning what your past life says about your life? Are you echoing what others say about your life? Or are you proclaiming what God says?

Today is a new day! Through Jesus and His work on the cross of Calvary, and your belief in that redemptive work, you are a new creation in Christ! You need to declare what God says about you, not what the kingdom of darkness or any other voice might say. You need to say, what God says about you, your family, your circumstances, your life, and your business.

In Romans 3:3-4, it states, *"For what if some did not believe? Will their unbelief make God's faith ineffective? God forbid: yes, let God be true, but every person a liar; as it is written, That you might be justified in your words, and might overcome when you are judged."*

We are encouraged by God to let His truth prevail and to speak what He has declared about us. This passage assures us that by embracing God's truth, we can triumph over the kingdom of darkness when it seeks to judge us. It provides us with a response and a saviour in the Lord Jesus Christ. We must allow Him and His Word to be true and actively engage His promises by repeatedly speaking His Word over our lives, families, and circumstances.

In James 3:2-10 it says:

"For in many things we offend everyone. If anyone does not offend in word, the same is a perfect person, and able also to control the whole body. Behold, we put bits in the horses' mouths, that they may obey us; and we turn about their whole body. Behold also the ships, which though they be so great, and are driven of fierce winds, yet are they turned about with a very small helm, wherever the governor lists. Even so the tongue is a little member, and boasts great things. Behold, how great a matter a little fire kindles! And the tongue is a fire, a world of iniquity: so is the tongue among our members, that it defiles the whole body, and sets on fire the course of nature; and it is set on fire of hell. For every kind of beasts, and of birds, and of serpents, and of things in the sea, is tamed, and hath been tamed of mankind: But the tongue can no man tame; it is an unruly evil, full of deadly poison. Therewith bless we God, even the Father; and therewith curse we men, which are made after the similitude of God. Out of the same mouth proceeds blessing and cursing. My brethren, these things ought not so to be."

The Secret Power Of The Tongue

In the preceding verses from the book of James, we find enlightening words about the power of the tongue. James compares the tongue's power to the rudder of a ship. Even though the ship is buffeted by strong winds, a small rudder can still steer it through life's storms.

As we study these verses, we see that God our Father challenges us to speak words of blessing. No one is perfect; we all make mistakes. That's why we can ask God to forgive us and apply the blood of Jesus to our burdens, allowing us to move away from them. We can start anew every day, even during the day! We can begin filling our hearts and minds with God's heart, worship, praise, until out of the abundance of our heart, our mouth speaks forth God's Word, life, love, and blessing.

We need to renew our mind with God's Word through meditation, speaking, and singing, filling our cars, homes, and the atmosphere around us with words of praise from God's own Word.

Just as you can direct a horse with a bridle and bit in its mouth, you can change direction by speaking the right words.

That's how powerful words are!

Chapter Nineteen:

If It's To Be, It's Up To Me!

"That the communication of your faith may become effectual by the acknowledging of every good thing which is in you in Christ Jesus."
— **Philemon 1:6**

Paul's words in Philemon 1:6 tells us that to communicate, share, and express our faith effectively, we must recognise every good thing within us in Christ Jesus. Our faith becomes effective as we acknowledge, communicate, and confess all the good things we now possess through the Kingdom Jesus Christ provided for us through His death and resurrection. 2 Corinthians 5:17 states, *"If any person is in Christ, he or she is a new creation; old things have passed away. Look, all things have become new!"*

Once you are born-again, you become a new creation, a type of being that never existed before. You are now a child of God! As the book of Luke 17:22 states, the Kingdom of God is within you. God reminds us not to forget but to remember that we are

His children, His Kingdom resides within us, and His Word is close to us. Romans 10:8-10 explains:

"But what say it? The Word is near you, even in your mouth, and in your heart: that is, the Word of faith, which we preach; That if you shall confess with your mouth the Lord Jesus, and shall believe in your heart that God has raised him from the dead, you shall be saved. For with the heart man believes unto righteousness; and with the mouth confession is made unto salvation."

These above verses highlight the significance of believing with our heart and confessing with our mouth what God's Word declares. By doing so, we recognise every good thing within us through Christ Jesus.

The Word continues in Romans 10:11-13 *"For the scripture says, Whosoever believes on him shall not be ashamed. For there is no difference between the Jew and the Greek: for the same Lord over all is rich unto all that call upon him. For whosoever shall call upon the name of the Lord shall be saved."*

If It's To Be, It's Up To Me!

I titled this chapter, *"If it's to be, it is up to me!"* Why? Because if I'm going to draw closer to God, it's up to me. James 4:8 in the Bible declares, *"Draw near to God, and He will draw near to you."* You can choose to respond to this verse in this way: *"I draw near to God, and He draw nears to me. If it's to be, it is up to me."*

Jesus promised, that, *"Blessed are those that hunger and thirst after righteousness, for they shall Be filled."* (Matthew 5:6). If it's to be, it is up to me. I must hunger, and I must thirst, then I shall be filled. Jesus also declared, *"Blessed are the merciful, for they shall obtain mercy."* (Matthew 5:7). If it's to be, it's up to me. I choose to be merciful, then I obtain mercy.

Do I desire the fulfilment of all my material needs? Food, drink, clothing, a home, or a place to live? If so, it's up to me to make it happen! These necessities have been provided for us through the great salvation that God offered through His Son's life, given on the cross. By giving and living according to the principles and keys of the Kingdom of God, God meets all our needs according to His riches in glory. In His Word, Romans 8:32, God assures us, *"He that spared not his own Son, but delivered him up for us all, how shall he not with him also freely give us all things?"*

God desires for you to enjoy life and experience your best life now. He promises in His Word that He provides us with all things richly to enjoy (1 Timothy 6:17). In 3 John 2, God expresses His primary wish for us, is to prosper and be in health as our soul prospers. Our Lord and Saviour Jesus, who is the Master of our lives, assured us of all the material necessities needed for a blessed life. In Matthew 6:33, Jesus said, *"But seek first the Kingdom of God and His righteousness, and all these things shall be added to you."*

Part of the Great Salvation that Romans 8:10 speaks about is having all of your needs met; both material, emotional and spiritual. How can we escape if we neglect such a great salvation? (Hebrews 2:3). The book of 2 Timothy 2:15 says, *"Study to show yourself approved unto God, a workman that needs not to be ashamed, rightly dividing the Word of truth."*

Study The Word

God desires for us to study His Word, praying that the Holy Spirit will grant us understanding and revelation. This is essential so we can comprehend the greatness of salvation and how to apply it in our lives, allowing us to experience its manifestation and enjoy the life God intended for us from the beginning. It cost God everything to give us the ability to live in and with His faith. As 2 Corinthians 8:9 states, *"For you know the grace of our Lord Jesus Christ, that though he was rich, yet for your sake he became poor, so that through his poverty you might become rich."*

On the cross, Jesus sacrificed everything for us. He carried our problems, sins, curses, and diseases in His own body. By the stripes He bore, we were healed. With His blood, we are redeemed and set free. We are now in covenant with God through the shed blood of the Lord Jesus Christ and our faith released in it.

If it's meant to be, it's up to me!

In Matthew 8:8, Jesus told the centurion soldier that he had never seen or found such great faith, not even in Israel. What was this *"great faith"*? The centurion soldier had said, *"Speak the word only, and my servant shall be healed."*

Do you want great faith? If so, it's up to you. You only need to speak the Word! Avoid talking about your problems, defeats, lack, or fears. Instead, focus on speaking the word. Say this right now, out loud: *"Death and life are in the power of my tongue. I choose life, that I may live and that my seed lives after me."*

Learn to express what you want, not what you have. Speak blessings instead of curses. Say what God says. In Romans 3:4, the Bible states: *"Let God be true and every man a liar."*

It's up to us to let God's Word be true in our lives. We must choose The Blessing by choosing the Word. We must choose the life by choosing Jesus Christ as our lord and saviour and be living in the great salvation that has been provided for us by His shed blood and life given at Calvary.

Abundance of Grace

In James 4:6, it states, *"But He gives more grace. Therefore He says, 'God opposes the proud but gives grace to the humble.'"* Do you desire God's gift of grace? Then say this: *"If it's meant to be, it depends on me!"* Declare, *"I humbly submit myself to the Lord and His Word."* Speak it, proclaim it, and most importantly, believe it in your heart. Trust that what you say will come true, and it will.

Jesus offers us an invitation in Matthew 11:28-30: *"Come to me, all you who labour and are burdened, and I will give you rest. Take my yoke upon you and learn from me, for I am gentle and humble in heart, and you will find rest for your souls. For my yoke is easy, and my burden is light."*

If it is to be, it is up to me. I come to Jesus now and declare, *"I receive His rest!"*

Do I long for abundant financial blessings? The key to the Lord's financial bounties is found in 2 Corinthians 9:6: *"But this I say: He who sows sparingly will also reap sparingly, and he who sows generously will also reap generously."*

There we have it! The Word tells us that I reap financially according to the measure that I sow. Do I truly desire abundance? Well, if it's to be, then it's up to me! I always sow generously, and God sees to it that I reap generously. The Bible tells us that God loves a prompt, quick-to-do-it giver, whose heart is in their giving, and they do it cheerfully and joyfully (2 Corinthians 9:7-9).

When we give, we bless someone else. When we give, we empower them to prosper or have a need met. When we give to a ministry, we empower that minister or ministry to extend the Kingdom and do the work of God. And God promises that every seed sown bears fruit after its own kind.

Luke 6:38 states, *"Give, and it shall be given unto you; good measure, pressed down, and shaken together, and running over, shall men give into your bosom. For with the same measure that you measure with it shall be measured to you again."*

Being poor is not a sin, though it can be very inconvenient. In Luke 4:18, Jesus mentioned that he came to bring good news to the poor. One way to break the cycle of poverty in our lives and families is by giving and being good stewards of the finances and resources God has entrusted to us.

Deuteronomy 8:17-18 says: *"And you say in your heart, My power and the might of mine hand has gotten me this wealth. 18 But you shall remember the Lord your God: for it is he that gives you power to get wealth, that he may establish his covenant which he swore unto your fathers, as it is this day."*

Freedom from financial worries is promised to us by God in His Word. Many people lose peace and joy because they constantly worry about money. However, for Christians, this should not be the case. God promises that if we are faithful in giving tithes and offerings and bring them into His storehouse, He will pour out great blessings upon our lives! (Malachi

3:10-12). In the same chapter, verse 11, God promises to rebuke the devourer for the sake of those who are obedient in tithes and offerings. God continues to say that the devourer will not destroy the fruit of our ground nor our vines in the field, but our seeds, vines, and fields, which represent our livelihoods, will not fail to bear fruit. In verse 12, God says that all the nations will call you blessed because you are a delightful land. In other words, God wants His people, His church, His faithful and obedient followers to be blessed. As we do His Word, we are blessed in the doing of it. It's what James 2:14-26 speaks about in the Bible when it tells us that our faith must have works, or corresponding actions. There has to be an action on our behalf that proves we have faith and demonstrates it. In Malachi 3:13, God says, *"Your words have been stout against me, says the LORD. Yet you say, What have we spoken so much against you?"*

Think about that for a moment. God says our words have been against Him. In the King James version, it uses an old English word—stout. Your words have been stout against me. You'd remember that we discussed this word earlier in the book, In the Hebrew, that word means to *"bind, conquer, and restrain."* God is showing us here in these verses, once again, how important the words of our mouth are. They must be aligned with and represent the faith that's in our hearts and the attitude that is in our soul.

Remember, God loves a cheerful giver, whose heart is in their giving and is prompt and obedient in their giving. In the Bible, God is telling us that we must speak words in line with our giving and in line with our tithes and offerings. God is revealing to us that our words can bind, restrain, and even conquer Him on our behalf in our life circumstances and matters.

You might wonder, *"How can my words conquer, restrain, or hinder God?"* They don't do so in His role as the sovereign ruler of the universe, Earth, and everything in it. However, your words can influence God's work on your behalf. They can prevent God from being the God He wants to be in your situation. Your words might also stop Him from bringing your victory into reality. Even the angels of God can be affected by your words if you speak the wrong thing.

As Psalms 103:20 states, *"Bless the LORD, you his angels, that excel in strength, that do his commandments, hearkening unto the voice of his Word."*

You were created in the image of God, reflecting His likeness, and empowered to operate with His God-kind of faith. Jesus said, have the faith of God. Speak to the mountain, speak to the problem, and command it to move out of your way and into the sea (Mark 11:23). Believe what you say with both your mouth and heart, and keep saying and believing it until you have it (Mark 11:24). Remember, with the heart, man believes, but with the mouth, confession is made unto salvation (Romans 10:10).

Empower Angels

The angels are listening for God's commands, because His Word is His commandments and it is His will. When you speak His Word and will concerning your life, family, business, and circumstances, you are aligning those things with God's Word and promises. According to Hebrews 1:14, the angels of God are set forth to minister on your behalf. These mighty beings of true light excel in strength, standing against forces of darkness, and causing God's promises to manifest and come to pass on your behalf.

So once again, God is giving us insight into the power of our words. We don't want our words to restrain or hinder God from working on our behalf. We don't want our words to restrain, conquer, or hinder the angels of God from working on our behalf.

We're want our words to empower the angelic forces! And we want our words to be in agreement with God and His Word! Because Jesus said, *"For where two or three are gathered together in my name, there am I in the midst of them"* (Matthew 18:20).

As mentioned earlier in this book, we don't want our words to tire God. Malachi 3:14 questions, *"you have said, It is vain to serve God: and what profit is it that we have kept his ordinance, and that we have walked mournfully before the LORD of hosts?"*

When we ask what benefit there is in keeping God's ordinances and then, instead of walking joyfully before Him, we begin to walk as mourners, worriers, and complainers, we are in trouble. If we start saying that people who don't serve God are more blessed than those who do, we place ourselves in a position where God cannot bless us. We enter a realm of unbelief, opposing His Word and will.

However, when we praise God and thank Him with a heart full of gratitude, believing His Word is true, and speak that word in faith, trusting that what we say will come to pass, with a joyful heart, Jesus says you can have what you say! *"Whatever you ask in my name, I will do, so that the Father may be glorified in the Son"* (John 14:23). However, this must originate from a trusting, loving, and joyful heart, not from bitterness and unbelief.

Malachi 3:16 states, *"Then those who feared the LORD spoke often to one another, and the LORD listened and heard it. A book of remembrance was written before Him for those who feared the LORD and thought upon His name."*

Heaven hears and records our conversations. The Lord listens to and hears the words we speak. Heaven is documenting in its book of remembrance all those who fear God and frequently speak of His name and Word.

God instructs us in the Bible to seek first His Kingdom and righteousness, assuring that all other necessary things will be added to us (Matthew 6:33). When Jesus spoke these words in the gospels, He was referring not only to spiritual matters but also to life's essentials: food, clothing, homes, cars, education, and jobs. This is to live a blessed life.

The Bible states in Luke 12:28, *"If then God so clothe the grass, which is today in the field, and tomorrow is cast into the oven; how much more will He clothe you, O you of little faith?"* If God cares for the grass, birds, and flowers, giving them colours, how much more will He surely take care of His children, whom He created in His own image? The Bible tells us in Galatians 3:29, *"And if you be Christ's, then are you Abraham's seed, and heirs according to the promise."*

God promised to bless Abraham and his descendants. He promised to provide for Abraham everything he needed, including finance, protection, shelter, food, and whatever would be considered a good life. God promised this for Abraham and his seed. Through Christ, you have become a seed of Abraham and have inherited the promise. This promise was of blessing, multiplication, and increase. It's the message of the gospel, the good news: God has wonderful and great things in store for our lives.

A God Designed Life

I have written this book, so that you by studying it, can receive this revelation on the secret power of the tongue. I pray, it will be birthed in your spirit by the Holy Spirit. Then you can begin to rise up in life through the Lord Jesus Christ. You can start to learn the principle of giving. And as you give, speak joyful, faith-filled words, like, *"Wow, it's more blessed to give than to receive!"* and *"Thank you, Jesus, for enabling me to bless that person's life! To make a difference in that person's life! Thank you, Jesus, for using me today to encourage, to put something positive, some faith, love, and even practical love, financially or however God leads, into the life of another person."*

God designed life to be given, shared, and not for people just to take. I like to say, *"Jesus Christ was and is the best Christmas present that ever was."* He's the gift you have received! The gift that never stops giving. He is the gift that keeps on giving and giving and giving. Remember, John 3:16 says, *"For God so loved the world, that he gave his only begotten Son, that whosoever believes in him should not perish, but have everlasting life."*

Here, is Don Gossett's *"never again"* list on *"giving and receiving."*

My Never Again List
by Don Gossett[3]

1. ***I am a tither!*** Never again will I confess God is closing the window of heaven to me. I pay my tithes and offerings and God promises, *"he will open heavens windows to my life"* (Malachi 3:10)

2. **I am someone who honours God!** Never again will I confess my life dishonours the Lord. Gladly, I will honour the Lord with my substance and first fruit of all my increase, my reward shall be plenty (Proverbs 3:9-10).

---
[3] The "*I AMs*" have been added by the author. (This list has been used with permission).

3. **I am a bountiful giver!** Never again will I confess I am not reaping as a result of my giving unto the Lord, God promises *"He who sows sparingly will reap sparingly He who reaps bountifully will reap bountifully"* (2 Corinthians 9:6).

4. **I am a cheerful giver!** Never again will I confess that God doesn't love me, God loves me! (John 3:16). For I am one of His children. He loves me especially because *"God loves a cheerful giver"* (2 Corinthians 9:7).

5. **I am an obedient giver!** Never again will I confess that God compels me to give, for the Bible says, *"not grudgingly or of necessity."* Rather, *"let every man give according to as he purposes in his heart"* (2 Corinthians 9:7).

6. **I am blessed!** Never again will I confess giving produces no blessing, *"I remember the words of the Lord Jesus Christ, how he said, it is more blessed to give than to receive"* (Act 20:35).

7. **I am delivered from the works and will of the devil!** Never again will I confess that my giving has no influence over the devil, God declares that when I prove him by giving my tithes and offering, that he *"rebukes the devourer [Satan] for my sake"* (Malachi 3:11).

8. **I am overflowing with abundance!** Never again will I confess my giving achieves no miracle. Give and it shall be given unto you! Good measure, pressed down, and shaken together, and running over, shall men give into your bosom. For with same measure you measure out, it shall be measured to you again (Luke :386).

9. **I am debt free!** Never again will I confess that if I give I will go deeper into debt. God declares, that if I *"withhold more than which is right it tends to poverty"* (Proverbs 11:24).

The law of confession is one of the most powerful truths I have discovered in the Bible. Romans 10:9-10 states: *"If you confess with your mouth that Jesus is Lord and believe in your heart that God raised him from the dead, you will be saved. For with the heart one believes unto righteousness, and with the mouth confession is made unto salvation."*

The essence of the Bible, the gospel message, the central truth of salvation, and all its benefits are received through this principle.

Salvation is both a heart and mouth experience. With our heart, we believe that the Lord Jesus Christ died for our sins. He was buried and went to hell on our behalf. On the third day, God raised Him from the dead through the grace and power of the Holy Spirit. We believe this in our heart and with our mouth we confess Jesus' Lordship over our life.

In the Book of Acts 8, we see an example of this salvation. Philip, the evangelist, preached to the Ethiopian eunuch about Jesus. Philip clearly expanded the gospel message to this Ethiopian man. As they traveled, they came to a certain body of water. The Ethiopian asked, *"Here is water. What hinders me from being baptised?"*

Philip responded with Romans 10:9-10: *"If you believe with all your heart, you may be baptised."* The Ethiopian replied, *"I believe Jesus Christ is the Son of God."* He was saved, and Philip baptised him there and then in that water!

Baptism in water is an outward sign of the inward grace that has taken place in a person's heart. For more teaching on this, please see my book, *"Life Changing Principles for Victorious Living"* (available through online book sellers).

Chapter Twenty:

Who I Am In Christ

"Christ in you the hope of glory"
— **Colossians 1:27**

The Word of God Says:

I AM…

- I am God's child for I am born again of incorruptible seed of the Word of God which liveth and abides forever (1 Peter 1:23).
- I am forgiven of all my sins and washed in the blood (Hebrews 9:14; Ephesians 1:7; Colossians 1:14; 1 John 2:12; 1:9).
- I am a new Creation in Christ (2 Corinthians 5:17)
- I am delivered From the power of darkness and translated into God's Kingdom (Colossians 1:13).
- I am redeemed from the curse of the law (1 Peter 1:18, Galatians 3:13).
- I am blessed (Deuteronomy 28:1-14, Galatians 3:9).

- I am a Saint (Romans 1:7, 1 Corinthians 1:2, Philippians 1:1).
- I am the head and not the tail (Deuteronomy 28:13).
- I am above only and not beneath (Deuteronomy 28:13).
- I am holy and without blame before Him in love (1 Peter 16, Ephesians. 1:4).
- I am elect (Colossians 3:12, Romans 8:33).
- I am established to the end (1 Corinthians 1:8).
- I am made nigh by the blood of Christ (Ephesians 2:13).
- I am victorious (Revelation 21:7).
- I am set free (John 8:31,32,33).
- I am strong in the Lord (Ephesians 6:10).
- I am dead to sin (Romans 6:2,11, 1 Peter 2:24).
- I am more than a conqueror (Romans 8:37).
- I am joint heirs with Christ (Romans 8:17).
- I am sealed with the Holy Spirit of Promise (Ephesians 1:13).
- I am in Christ Jesus by His doing (1 Corinthians 1:30).
- I am accepted in the beloved (Ephesians 1:6).
- I am complete in Him (Colossians 2:1).

Who I Am In Christ

- I am crucified with Christ (Galatians 2:20).
- I am alive with Christ (Ephesians 2:5).
- I am free from condemnation (Romans 8:1)
- I am reconciled to God (2 Corinthians 5:18).
- I am qualified to share His inheritance (Colossians 1:12).
- I am firmly rooted, built up, established in my faith and overflowing with gratitude (Colossians 2:7).
- I am a fellow citizen with the saints and of the household of God (Ephesians 2:19).
- I am built upon the foundation of the apostles and prophets, Jesus Christ Himself being the chief (Ephesians 2:20).
- I am a cornerstone (Ephesians 2:20).
- I live like Jesus in the world (1 John 4:17).
- I am born of God and the evil one does not touch me (1 John 5:18).
- I am His faithful follower (Revelation 17:14, Ephesians 5:1).
- I am overtaken with blessings (Deuteronomy 28:2, Ephesians 1:3).
- I am His disciple because I have a love for others (John 13:34-25).

- I am the light of the world (Matthew 5:14).
- I am the salt of the Earth (Matthew 5:13).
- I am the righteousness of God (2 Corinthians 5:21, 1 Peter 2:24).
- I am a partaker of is divine nature (2 Peter 1:4).
- I am called of God (2 Timothy 1:9).
- I am the first fruits among His creation (James 1:18).
- I am chosen (1 Thessalonians 1:4, Ephesians 1:4, 1 Peter 2:9).
- I am an ambassador for Christ (2 Corinthians 5:20).
- I am God's workmanship created in Christ Jesus for good works (Ephesians 2:10).
- I am the apple of my Father's eye (Deuteronomy 32:10, Psalm 17:8).
- I am healed by the stripes of Jesus (1 Peter 2:24, Isaiah 53:6).
- I am being changed into His image (2Corinthians 3:18, Philippians 1:6).
- I am raised up with Christ and seated in Heavenly places (Colossians 2:12, Ephesians 2:6).
- I am beloved of God (Colossians 3:12, Romans 1:7, 1 Thessalonians 1:4).

Who I Am In Christ

- I am one in Christ (John 17:21-23).

I HAVE…

- I have the mind of Christ (Philippians 2:5, 1 Corinthians 2:16).
- I have obtained an inheritance (Ephesians 1:11).
- I have access by one Spirit unto the Father (Hebrews 4:16, Ephesians 2:18).
- I have overcome the World (1 John 5:4).
- I have everlasting life and will not be condemned (John 5:24, 6:47).
- I have the peace of God which passes understanding (Philippians 4:7).
- I have received power, the power of the Holy Spirit (Acts 1:8).
- I have power to lay hands on the sick and see them recover (Mark 16:18).
- I have power to cast out demons (Mark 16:17).
- I have power over all the power of the enemy, and nothing shall by any means hurt me (Mark 16:17-18, Luke 10:17,19).

I LIVE…

- I live by and in the law of the Spirit of life in Christ Jesus (Romans 8:2).

I WAIK…

- I walk in Christ Jesus (Colossians 2:6).

I CAN…

- I can do all things through Christ, who strengthens me (Philippians 4:13).

MY LIFE…

- My life is hid with Christ in God (Colossians 3:3).

I SHALL…

- I shall do even greater works than Christ Jesus (John 14:12).

I POSSESS…

- I possess the greater one in me because greater is He who is in me than he who is in the world (1 John 4:4).

I PRESS...

- I press towards the goal of the prize of the high calling of God in Christ Jesus (Philippians 3:1).

I FORGET...

- I forget what lies behind and I read towards the things that are up ahead (Philippians 3:12-14).

I ALWAYS...

- I always triumph in Christ (2 Corinthians 2:14).
- I always show forth His praise (1 Peter 2:9).

I REMEMBER...

- I remember it is God who gives me the power to get wealth that His covenant may be established in the land.

The Secret Power Of The Tongue

Chapter Twenty-One:

Daily Affirmations

"You shalt also decree a thing, and it shall be established unto you: and the light shall shine upon your ways."
— Job 22:28

I have included some personal affirmations here to help you succeed in life through Jesus Christ. I believe that your personal empowerment in Jesus Christ comes as you acknowledge—as we've discussed in this book—every good thing that is in you through Christ Jesus. The word *"affirm"* means to *"make firm."* An affirmation is a statement of truth that strengthens you in that truth through repetition. We are instructed in the Bible in Titus 3:8 to *"affirm constantly these things."*

In Hebrews 10:23, we are instructed to *"Let us hold fast the confession of our faith without wavering, for He who has promised is faithful."*

Affirming the promises in God's Word strengthens your faith and its effectiveness. Your faith is meant to produce specific outcomes, and these become powerful when affirmed. The Bible highlights positive thinking, as we've discussed, but it also emphasises the power of words. Why? Words gain strength through volume, emotion, conviction, and enthusiasm. Mark Twain famously said, *"I was born enthusiastic."*

Embrace enthusiasm for God and His Word, and apply it to your life. Incorporate affirmations into your daily routines. The book of Job states that if you declare something, it will be established for you! (Job 22:28).

Speak aloud the following affirmations, if possible, at the beginning of every day until you you write your own or others. Bring God's Word and illumination into your life and daily routine by spreading forth what the Word says!

Daily Affirmations of Life and Victory

- This is the day that the Lord has made; I will rejoice and be glad in it! (Psalm 118:24)

- Today, I choose love instead of fear. I choose peace instead of conflict. I choose to be a love-finder instead of a fault-finder. I choose to be a love-giver instead of a love-seeker. What I give, I will receive. What I sow, I shall reap.

Daily Affirmations

- I will bless the Lord at all times; His praise shall continually be in my mouth. (Psalm 34:1)

- I feel healthy. I feel happy. I feel terrific! I am fantastic and getting better every day! (Repeat 3x)

- I can do all things through Christ who strengthens me. (Philippians 4:13)

- I am a man/woman of God. He has cleansed me by the blood of Jesus Christ. My Father has filled me with His Spirit. I am dedicated to the Lord Jesus, strong and powerful in Him. I worship and serve Him with all the divine energy He inspires within me.

- Greater is He who is in me than he who is in the world. (1 John 4:4)

- I am humble, strong, courageous, full of faith, and powerful in the Lord.

- If God is for me, who can be against me? (Romans 8:31)

- I am a child of God. My Father has adopted me into His family. He has moved me out of darkness into the light of His Kingdom. God's protective shield is around me. I have angelic protection, and He is providing every need in my life.

- My God shall supply all my needs according to His riches in glory by Christ Jesus. (Philippians 4:19)

- Every day, in every way, by the grace of God, I am getting better and better! I have a positive mindset, speak words of faith, and take disciplined action.

- I am a doer of the Word, not just a hearer. (James 1:22)

- God has not given me a spirit of fear but of power, love, and a sound mind. (2 Timothy 1:7)

- God has forgiven me, and I have forgiven myself.

- The anointing of the Holy One abides in me. (1 John 2:27)

- My generous Father has blessed me with an abundant life. I am grateful, and I enjoy giving my time, talent, money, and love to others.

- He was wounded for my transgressions, bruised for my iniquities; surely He has borne our sorrows, and by His stripes, I am healed. (Isaiah 53:4-5)

- God loves me with unconditional love. I love God with all my heart, soul, mind, and strength. Because of His love, I am free to love myself and my neighbour.

Daily Affirmations

- We overcome the enemy by the blood of the Lamb and the word of our testimony, and we do not love our lives to the death. (Revelation 12:11)

- I belong to Jesus! I am friendly, strong, happy, and victorious. Everything is working out for my good!

- Rejoice in the Lord always. Again, I say, rejoice! (Philippians 4:4)

- God has given me a strong body, a sharp mind, and a vibrant spirit. I am talented, gifted, and a hard worker. I will achieve my goals.

- The Lord is the strength of my life; of whom shall I be afraid? (Psalm 27:1)

- God loves me, so I love Him. I trust Him with my life and will faithfully serve Him all my days.

- I am casting all my cares upon Him, for He cares for me. (1 Peter 5:7)

- God is my loving Father. He has given me a Saviour, His Son, Jesus Christ. He has given me His Holy Spirit. I have a healthy body, a sound mind, and material abundance. I live in a beautiful world, surrounded by many friends, and I am thankful for every blessing He has given me.

- I am the seed of Abraham through Jesus Christ, and Abraham's blessing rests upon me, my family, and my life. I am grateful, I am thankful, and I am full of praise to my God for His love and for all the blessings He pours into my life daily.

My prayer is that you will use this book as a powerful tool to defeat the devil and his attacks in your life, your family, your work, your business, or whatever the case may be. I pray that as you study this word it will be the beginning of a new walk for you as you learn to enjoy the secret power that is in your own tongue. That you will begin to enjoy the best life that God has for you.

This book is not an exhaustive book on the power of tongue or words. It is an introduction to it. I encourage you, the reader, to make a life-long study of this topic. Referring to this book often. I also encourage you to read the Bible from cover-to-cover, underlining verses, scriptures, and words that stand-out to you! There are many other authors that have written much on this topic of the tongue and the power of your imagination. I have mentioned my friend, Don Gossett (now in Glory), but other great works have been produced by authors such as: Kenneth Hagen, Kenneth Copeland, Jesse Duplantis, Jerry Savelle, E.W. Kenyan and many others.

Studying their works and the works of others on this topic will only expand and reinforce your understanding of this powerful revelation that will empower you to win in life through Jesus Christ.

God bless,
Shaun Marler.

The Secret Power Of The Tongue

A Guide to Salvation

1. Acknowledge Your Need for Salvation

Recognise that you cannot save yourself. No amount of good works can earn salvation—it is a gift from God.

2. Understand That God Has Made a Way

God has already done everything necessary for your salvation by giving His Son, Jesus Christ, to die for you. His sacrifice on the cross paid the price for your sins.

3. Believe in Jesus' Resurrection

The Bible tells us that if you believe in your heart that God raised Jesus from the dead, you will be saved (Romans 10:9). His resurrection is proof that He has conquered sin and death for you.

4. Confess Jesus as Lord

Salvation comes when you declare with your mouth, *"Jesus is Lord,"* and surrender your life to Him. This is a public declaration of your faith and trust in Him.

5. Be Baptised and Partake in Communion

Now that you are saved, follow Jesus' example by being baptised in water as an outward sign of your new life in Christ. Also, regularly take part in Holy Communion, remembering His sacrifice for you.

6. Be Filled with the Holy Spirit

Jesus promised that His followers would receive the Holy Spirit. Ask God to fill you with His Spirit, just as the early believers were filled in the Bible. Speaking in tongues is one of the signs of this infilling.

7. Love and Praise Jesus Daily

Though you have never seen Jesus, you love Him. Worship Him often, thanking Him for His goodness and greatness in your life.

8. Join a Bible-Believing Church

It is important to find and join a fellowship of believers who follow the whole truth of God's Word. Surround yourself with like-minded Christians who will encourage and strengthen your faith.

9. Stay Under Godly Leadership

As believers, we grow best when we fellowship together under the guidance of a pastor or shepherd who follows Jesus and teaches His Word faithfully.

10. Trust in God's Plan for Your Life

God has wonderful things in store for you. Giving your heart to Jesus is just the beginning of an incredible journey of faith, success, and purpose. Your best days are ahead! As Ecclesiastes 7:8 says, *"Better is the end of a thing than the beginning thereof."*

A final word from the author...

Jesus Loves You!

"The thief comes only to steal and kill and destroy; I have come that they may have life, and have it to the full." John 10:10 (NIV).

You are very special. GOD LOVES YOU. He sent His son Jesus Christ who died for you and was raised from the dead. You are a somebody because you were created by God and He doesn't make nobodies.

You are God's best, His dream, His idea.

"For I know the plans I have for you," declares the Lord, "plans to prosper you and not to harm you, plans to give you hope and a future. Then you will call upon me and come and pray to me, and I will listen to you. You will seek me and find me when you seek me with all your heart. I will be found by you, declares the Lord..." Jeremiah 29:11-14 (NIV).

What Does God Say?

ROMANS 3:23 "For all have sinned and fall short of the glory of God."

A Final Word From The Author

ROMANS 6:23 "The wages of sin is death, but the gift of God is eternal life in Christ Jesus our Lord."

JOHN 3:16 "For God so loved the world that He gave His only begotten Son, that whosoever believes in Him should not perish but have everlasting life."

ACTS 4:12 "Nor is there salvation in any other name under heaven given among men by which we must be saved."

TITUS 3:5 "Not by works of righteousness which we have done, but according to His mercy He saved us…"

1 JOHN 1:9 "If we confess our sins He is faithful and just to forgive us our sins and cleanse us from all unrighteousness."

2 CORINTHIANS 5:21 "For He made Him who knew no sin to be sin for us, that we might become the righteousness of God in Him."

ROMANS 10:9-10 "That if you confess with your mouth the Lord Jesus and believe in your heart that God has raised Him from the dead, you will be saved. For with the heart one believes unto righteous-ness, and with the mouth confession is made unto salvation."

Remember, Keep Your Eyes on Jesus!

Seek first the Kingdom of God and His righteousness. Keep your lamp filled (your life, heart and mind) by staying in the Word and prayer. Live life-ready, by being obedient, submitted and led by the Holy Spirit. Be quick to forgive and quick to repent if you make a mistake. Get up and get going for God again. Stay in fellowship with other Christians and your local church where possible. Know that God has not appointed you to the day of His wrath and judgement but to obtain salvation, through our Lord Jesus Christ.

Salvation Prayer

Here is a simple prayer you can pray in order to be born again:

Father, I come before you in the precious name of Jesus.
Lord, I have made mistakes in my life.
Father, I acknowledge that I have sinned.
I see in Your Word it says that Jesus died for my sins.
Please forgive me of all of my sins and mistakes against you that I have committed, or any other person that I may have wronged.
I forgive all those who have sinned against me or wronged me in any way.
Father, I repent right now of my sins.

A Final Word From The Author

Father, I thank You that You sent Jesus, who came in the flesh and died for me, taking my sins on the cross, shedding His blood for me. Thank you, I am now clean from my sins, through the shed blood of Jesus Christ. Thank you that on the third day You rose Jesus again from the dead.
Jesus now sits at Your right hand in all power and glory, as King and Lord of all.
Jesus, please come into my life, my heart, right now by the Person and power of the Holy Spirit, and make me born again.
Jesus, I receive You now as my Lord and my Saviour. Amen.

Welcome to God's Family

Welcome to the family of God! Keep seeking Him, and He will lead you into His perfect plan for your life. If you prayed this simple prayer, you can know, according to God's Word that you are saved. You are now born again and have become a Christian, a follower of Christ. You must stand on His Word, not your feelings, emotions, or anything else. It is God's Word that guarantees your salvation.

Assurance of Salvation

"And this is the record that God has given to us eternal life, and this life is in His Son. HE THAT HAS THE SON HAS LIFE, and he that has not the Son of God has not life. These things have I written unto you that believe on the name of the Son of God; THAT YOU MAY KNOW that ye have eternal life, and that ye may BELIEVE ON THE NAME of the Son of God." (1 John 5: 11-13).

If you have made a decision for Jesus or if you have more questions about it, please email us!

newbelievers@whm.org.au

A Final Word From The Author

Footnotes

The following is a list of resources and sources, read and studied in the preparation of this book. Plus, further thankyous and acknowledgements to individuals who have had an impact on my life. Their thoughts, prayers and inspiration (some of which I have included in this work) have helped mould me, enlighten my thinking and inspired me to grow and touch this world for Christ.

'*The Amplified Bible,*' Jointly published by Zondervan and The Lockman Foundation.
Bible Hub. biblehub.com

'*Charting Your Course,*' by Robert Tilton.

'*Dake Annotated Reference Bible*,' Published by Dake's Publishing Inc.

'*Does Your Tongue Need Healing?*' By Derek Prince.
Google Dictionary.

'*God's Creative Power Will Work For You,*' by Charles Capps.

'*God's Will For Your Healing*,' by Gloria Copeland.
'*The King James Bible.*'

'*Nelson's Illustrated Bible Dictionary*,' by Thomas Nelson Publishers.

'*The NIV Bible,*' published by Zondervan in the United States and Hodder & Stoughton in the UK.

'*Power Series*,' by Drummond R. Thom.

'*Strong's Concordance*,' published by Thomas Nelson Publishers.

'*The Good Life*,' by T.L. Osborn.

'*The King's Decree*,' by Jodie Hughes.

'*The New Bible Dictionary*,' by Inter-varsity Fellowship.

'*The Power of Your Words*,' by Don Gossett and E.W. Kenyon.

'*The Winning Attitude*,' by Kenneth Copeland.

'*What You Say, Is What You Get,*' by Don Gossett.

'*You Can Have What You Say*,' by Kenneth E. Hagin.

About The Author

Dr Shaun Marler is the Senior Pastor and co-founder with his wife Kerrie of World Harvest Ministries, an international organisation based in Queensland, Australia, World Harvest Ministries is committed to carrying out the Great Commission of Jesus our Lord. Taking the healing word to the nations and feeding the hungry, visiting prisoners, clothing the naked, visiting the widows and orphans in their affliction, and preaching the Good News to the poor.

World Harvest Ministries currently has programs in Australia, Africa and India, where the poor and destitute are given free medical treatment, orphan homes where children are fed, accommodated and educated, a ministry to widows who have been abandoned by society and a program to feed people with leprosy.

World Harvest Ministries also works within their local greater Brisbane community, through Harvest Food Assist. With the help of volunteers, and the Harvest Care Team, we provide meals, clothes, blankets and share the Good News of the Gospel through these weekly outreaches.

A portion of the proceeds of the sale of this book goes towards this valuable work, which is making a huge difference in the lives of others!

Previous Books

Secret Place Living

Packed full of 'power thoughts' designed to empower you to win in life. The Bible says that out of the abundance of the heart, the mouth speaks. Thoughts are so powerful. What we meditate on today is creating the reality of our tomorrow.

The Rapture Of The Church

This book will help you prepare for the next great event on the Christian calendar. Learn what the word 'rapture' means — God's ability to catch up people alive to His presence. Timelines included, pointing to when we can expect this event to occur and much more!

Praise Power

Everything in your life is subject to change. God's Will for your life is that it changes for the better. How do you get there? Through praise in the word, because praise is the verbal expression of faith and faith is a language of heaven.

Divine Healing 101

This is how to book with examples, teachings and personal testimonies, that prove it is God's will that you not only be healed, but walk in divine health, all the days of your life.

Life Changing Principles For Victorious Living

Life changing principles for victorious living is a must read! You'll find keys to unlock your life in Christ.

The Fast Way To Power

Learn the secret to the presence and power of God, in the lives of some of His great generals. You'll learn the ABCs they knew that enable them to walk in God's miracle healing power.

Born Again: What Does It Really Mean?

This mini book is a must have! You will learn how you can accept Jesus Christ as saviour and what it really means to be born again. Discover how you can enjoy all the blessings that will now belong to you!

Partnership

Help Pastor Shaun to help others, by becoming a Harvest Partner in this great work of spreading the gospel and loving others.

Please email general@whm.org.au and become a World Harvest partner today!

For other information and a complete list of products, or to find out how you can partner with the ministry of Dr Shaun Marler and World Harvest Ministries, contact:

P.O. Box 90, Bald Hills, 4036
Queensland, Australia
Phone: +61 7 3261 4555
(9am - 4:30pm EST Aust)

Web: whm.org.au
Email: general@whm.org.au

Facebook: www.facebook.com/worldharvestmin
Facebook: www.facebook.com/ShaunMarlerWHM
X (formerly Twitter): twitter.com/world_harvest
Youtube: youtube.com/worldharvestlife
Instagram: @i_harvest

Notes

Notes

Notes

Notes

Notes

Notes

www.ingramcontent.com/pod-product-compliance
Lightning Source LLC
Chambersburg PA
CBHW031241290426
44109CB00012B/383